The Teaching of Ethics IV

Teaching Bioethics: Strategies, Problems, and Resources

K. Danner Clouser

INSTITUTE OF
SOCIETY, ETHICS AND
THE LIFE
SCIENCES THE
HASTINGS
CENTER

The Hastings Center
Institute of Society, Ethics and the Life Sciences
360 Broadway
Hastings-on-Hudson, New York 10706

Library of Congress Cataloging in Publication Data

Clouser, K Danner
    Teaching bioethics.

    (The Teaching of ethics ; 4)
    Bibliography: p.
    1. Medical ethics—Study and teaching. I. Title.
II. Series: Teaching of ethics ;4.
R724.C53   174′.2′0711   80–10492
ISBN 0–916558–07–X

Contents

FOREWORD

A concern for the ethical instruction and formation of students has always been a part of American higher education. Yet that concern has by no means been uniform or free of controversy. The centrality of moral philosophy in the undergraduate curriculum during the mid-nineteenth century gave way later during that century to the first signs of increasing specialization of the disciplines. By the middle of the twentieth century, instruction in ethics had, by and large, become confined almost exclusively to departments of philosophy and religion. Efforts to introduce ethics teaching in the professional schools and elsewhere in the university often met with indifference or outright hostility.

The past decade has seen a remarkable resurgence of interest in the teaching of ethics at both the undergraduate and professional school levels. Beginning in 1977, The Hastings Center, with the support of the Rockefeller Brothers Fund and the Carnegie Corporation of New York, undertook a systematic study of the teaching of ethics in American higher education. Our concern focused on the extent and quality of that teaching, and on the main possibilities and problems posed by widespread efforts to find a more central and significant role for ethics in the curriculum.

As part of that project, a number of papers, studies, and monographs were commissioned. Moreover, in an attempt to gain some degree of consensus, the authors of those studies worked together as a group for a period of two years. The study presented here represents one outcome of the project. We hope and believe it will be helpful for those concerned to advance and deepen the teaching of ethics in higher education.

Daniel Callahan   Sissela Bok
Project Co-Directors
The Hastings Center
Project on the Teaching of Ethics

About the Author

K. Danner Clouser

K. Danner Clouser is Professor of Humanities (Philosophy) at the Pennsylvania State University College of Medicine, Hershey, Pa. He graduated from Gettysburg College and the Lutheran Theological Seminary and received an M.A. and Ph.D. in Philosophy from Harvard. Subsequently, he taught philosophy at Dartmouth and Carleton colleges before joining the medical faculty of Pennsylvania in 1968. Since that time he has taught, lectured, and written in the fields of biomedical ethics and philosophy of medicine and has been active in developing the role of the humanities disciplines in medical education. Professor Clouser was an Associate Editor of the *Encyclopedia of Bioethics* and is on the editorial board of the *Journal of Medicine and Philosophy*.

Preface

During the last ten years, and particularly in the last five, a surprising phenomenon has taken place. There has been an incredible surge of interest in biomedical ethics. Workshops and conferences are widely offered and enthusiastically attended; medicine and science journals are publishing articles and editorials on ethics; traditional forums of medicine are presenting moral concerns; ethics courses offered by medical schools have increased a hundredfold, and undergraduate colleges many times that; societies, associations, and journals have been created for the advancement of the field; books and articles abound; foundations and government have given massive financial support.

Had this been going on for only two or three years, we might call it a fad. But its still increasing vigor after ten years qualifies it at least for "significant trend," and perhaps even for "major educational rediscovery." Even in these recent years of stringent budgetary cutbacks (especially in medical schools) the programs in medical ethics have continued to grow. In truth, the movement never did have the earmarks of being a mere fad. Its concerns were too important, too deep; it struck at questions and beliefs too profound to be trivialized or forgotten. Obviously, attention to biomedical ethics is resonating with something deep inside us.

Why this phenomenon has occurred, and why it occurred when it did, are puzzles best left in the hands of those sociohistorical experts who are equipped for constructing such explanations. Has it really been by virtue of our vastly increased technological ability to affect and control lives? Has something recalled professionals to the sources of their obligation to the public? Have we an intuitive awareness of the social abyss we face, if trust among humans continues to disintegrate?

Rather than explaining the surge of interest, the point of this monograph is to document it and, more important, to suggest ways of channeling it, to show that bioethics is doable, reasonable, and essential. The purpose is not to package and peddle courses; instead it is to show what is being done, present the variety of settings, the richness of possibilities, the available resources, and thus to stimulate the reader's imagination as to what might be done wherever one finds oneself. If along the way, in seeing the goals, possibilities, excitement, challenges, and importance, the reader is inspired to do more—that's even better. The concerns of bioethics speak to the essence of profession, of public trust, of life's quality, and of our very humanity. It is territory that we sense intensely must be regained.

"Regain" seems just the right word. As long as there have been therapies and healers there has been moral concern about the acquisition and use of this special knowledge, and the obligations between the healer and the client. Codes and covenants have evolved in all traditions; sometimes for protection of the patient, sometimes for the protection of the practitioner. It is as though human beings have intuitively sensed the intimacy, sensitivity, dependence, and dramatic importance of the therapeutic process and relationship, and therefore have structured and surrounded it with guiding rules.

Interest in medical ethics has waxed and waned throughout the centuries and in every culture. In our Western tradition occasionally a new statement, a new manifesto, a new formulation from the medical world has rekindled interest. However, most of the work on these issues has come from the religious traditions, particularly the Roman Catholic and the Jewish, which have searched and interpreted their own religious foundations and writings for implications relevant to the moral issues of medicine. The explicit teaching of "morals and medicine" has been kept alive in religious seminaries more than in medical schools. It was (and is) generally assumed that the ethics of medicine was learned by professionals during their apprenticeship to a senior physician. Hence, it was seldom taught explicitly in the medical classroom (except in some Roman Catholic medical schools where such courses have continued to be taught, usually by someone trained in moral theology).

There may have been an additional damper on teaching it in the medical school classroom. Very likely, the Flexnerian era (1910 and after) in medical education so stressed the science of medicine and the need for medical specialists to teach it, that ethics (1) was dropped as part of the unscientific aspects of medicine; (2) fell between the cracks of the specialities; (3) lost even its experiential exposure as the apprenticeship lost its centrality in education.

The present resurgence, now roughly in its tenth year, is much more than a replaying of what has gone before. Formal courses and other emphases in medical ethics now exist in the majority of medical schools in the country. Nursing and allied health professions are building such courses; and this is also true for other nonmedical professional schools and undergraduate colleges. Biomedical ethics has thus become a field for explicit study and scholarly focus; it is reaching patient, practitioner, and policy maker. It is not a new field, but the pervasiveness, enthusiasm, and educational formats are brand new; they comprise a movement with which the educator must come to terms.[1]

I. Introduction

This monograph has a variety of purposes which must be kept distinct. It is variously an essay, a documentary, a survey, an evaluation. If the reader is not to be misled, these different functions must be clearly labeled as they occur.

Further complicating this, like a multifactorial matrix, is the variety of educational settings with respect to which each report, observation, opinion, plea, and so on should be made. Our domain for consideration is no less than the teaching of biomedical ethics in medical schools, in nursing schools, in allied health schools, in graduate schools, in professional schools, and in undergraduate schools. The proliferation of detail in such a format would be exceeded only by the possibility of absolute boredom with such an account. Deliberating on every item—methods, topics, goals, training of teachers, student attitudes, evaluation, and so on—with respect to each school setting would be torturous beyond the bounds of decency. The reader would be adrift on such a sea of details—largely repetitious—that the highlights and important differences would be lost, as would the inspiration to teach. This document must aim for a place on that acreage between a plodding, overworked, endlessly specific government report and the zealous testimonial of an undergraduate teacher who has just discovered bioethics.

Three tactics will help us occupy that center ground. (a) We will use as our paradigm the teaching of ethics in medical schools. (b) We will begin impressionistically on a descriptive level, and only after that will we stand back to analyze the constituent elements, strategies, assumptions, and maneuvers. (c) Then we will briefly look at other educational settings to compare and contrast salient features of those settings with our paradigm case.

Once we have worked over the rather direct matters and methods and goals of teaching biomedical ethics, we will focus on some of the more controversial issues in and around the teaching of bioethics (as distinguished from the substantive issues of the field itself, which are not of direct concern here).

Finally, we will deal with the more empirical matters: what is actually being taught, where and how; and the resources available for teachers of bioethics.

II. The Paradigm

A. The Point

A further word of explanation for the use of the "paradigm" is necessary. Inasmuch as we will deal here with a variety of professional educational settings, it would seem that clarity is to be gained and confusion diminished by dealing with one setting thoroughly (the paradigm) and then calling attention to the significant differences in the other settings. Beginning with a particular instead of with abstractions and their variations and qualifiers, seems the better road to understanding. Furthermore, the manner of presenting the paradigm is important. It should not get bogged down in details and discussion. It needs to convey quickly a mood, a process, a strategy, a feel for the pressures, constraints, and focuses of the medical school setting, and also for what happens in a classroom in that context. It is an impressionistic sketch meant to draw us into the realities of the situation. That done, we will stand back to reflect on the pedagogical components manifested there, along with other possibilities and considerations.

B. The Setting

Medical students are very anxious to become professionals. They are eager to identify with medicine. They seek enthusiastically that which is uniquely different from their undergraduate training, whatever will suggest to themselves and to others that they are now in medicine. Much of their first two years of medical school seems to them depressingly like a continuation of college—more biochemistry, more behavioral sciences, more microbiology and genetics. Where is the *essence* of their chosen career? Gross anatomy (and its heavy schedule of laboratory work, dissecting cadavers) at least is significantly different from any of their previous training and seems to bespeak a trust and tradition unique to medical students. Any offered elective in those first two years, such as in emergency medicine or first aid, will be hungrily enrolled in by many students. (After all, what student wants to be home on vacation, known by the neighborhood to be a medical student, and yet in a crisis be outperformed by the local Boy/Girl Scout.) In short, there is considerable eagerness to establish a professional identity, to make significant contact with the heart of one's career. Conversely, there is much impatience with those enterprises that do not make such contact.

By and large, medical students are very bright. They quickly see points, lines of reasoning, and implications. However, there are generally two characteristics of their training that need to be identified and dealt with. (1) They have gone lockstep through the sciences as undergraduates. They are accustomed to large classes, taking in huge amounts of information, learning it, and answering multiple-choice questions about it. (2) They tend to see the world of education or learning as a dichotomy. There is "hard" science, and then there is everything else. The latter is "soft," impressionistic, opinionated, uncertain, highly subjective. Science, on the other hand, is true; there are right answers; one has only to learn it and apply it, and if it were not for the "soft" disciplines mucking up situations, everything would be well.

These are not usually points of contention. Indeed, unless students are pressed, these points are seldom explicitly articulated. Rather, the two characteristics constitute a kind of deep-seated orientation of the students (and more likely, of the medical center at large), and are something the teacher of these students should be aware of and use to educational advantage. Obviously, part of the implication of this orientation is that the students do not really understand science. They have a kind of rote knowledge of it, but little appreciation of its creativity, methodology, assumptions, controversies, and pitfalls. Their imaginations have not been stimulated; their critical abilities have not been honed.

The context of the medical school into which these students are thrust strongly reinforces the deep-seated orientation just described. Information overkill is delivered in very large lecture classes; classes tightly fill the day from 8:00 A.M. to 5:00 P.M. There is no time for deliberation, no time for understanding. Students spend all day being lectured to and all evening reading thick handouts and enormous textbooks. Students seem to experience little satisfaction in learning, although they are in general the kind of persons who would enjoy pursuing, questioning, delving, and understanding. (Actually, they did more of that as undergraduates.) Ordinarily graduate work is an opportunity for work in depth, but it does not seem so in this context.

The setting is, in fact, a kind of "conceptual ghetto," and seems to reflect the setting of all professional schools, not just medicine. When the same presuppositions, purposes, and points of interest are shared by a community, it is as though they are locked into a ghetto. Their view of themselves, others, their relationships, goals, and desiderata are the same. A severely limited perspective is fostered. Furthermore, as might be expected, this perspective is reinforced throughout their training: in language, terminology, rewards, and direction of attention. There is a directive toward reductionism: what is the underlying biochemical mechanism? There is a premium on what is new and different: is the patient an "interesting" case? There is a focus on the quantifiable and a reliance on the technological to the point of ignoring that to which a number cannot be assigned or that to which no instrument relates, to the point of effectively denying the existence of that on which there is no "hard data."[2] Even the success of a therapy is ultimately measured in the quantity of life days gained, rather than the quality of those days.[3]

The notion of a "conceptual ghetto," only vaguely hinted at here, is not mentioned as criticism (it has important advantages as well as disadvantages) but only as a phenomenon to be bargained with by an educator. And indeed the difference between the direction, focuses, content, and method of ethics and that of the context just described can be effectively symbolized and capitalized on by going counter to the standard medical-course format. Small classes with in-depth, head-to-head discussion seem called for. The material of ethics cannot be appropriately dealt with when it is treated as just so much more information to be recorded in notebooks. Instead, it must work its way into the student's consciousness, so he or she can use it, interact with it, argue with it and become sensitive to it.

C. The Paraphrased Class Discussion

We leap immediately to the paraphrasing of several likely class discussions. It seems precipitous, but we have our reasons. Many heated discussions about aspects of teaching ethics have taken place. One often suspects that the matter is being argued in abstractions which bear little resemblance to anything one has seen go on in a classroom, and that an understanding might be quickly reached if those concerned could be together in a classroom to see what actually is happening. Is the student being manipulated? Is it sheer indoctrination? Is it just one person's subjectivity over against another's? Can anyone in a profession teach the ethics of that profession?

What follows is no substitute for being part of a class; it may not even be helpful. But it is worth a try. No attempt will be made to present it as a dialogue, but it will reveal broadly the subtopics and their rough sequence as they might well, and frequently do, occur in a classroom. The purpose is to assist us in thinking ourselves into the classroom situation in the hope of being stimulated toward more appropriate and realistic ideas, observations, and insights into the teaching of professional ethics. Here are some sample topics and a very likely sequence of issues unfolding from them.

1. Orientation

The first day of class is often an open discussion about why the students chose this course and what they hope to get out of it. Inevitably a number will suggest that they expect to be told how to behave better. Others, or the instructor, will ask that group if simply receiving a list of rules to follow would satisfy them. The answer is always no, but they are not sure why. So the class explores those reasons, and then the nature of those reasons. Are these "reasons" different in moral matters from other kinds of matters? are they like "reasons" for deciding on a diagnosis and therapy—which, after all, have to do with behavior? Are these "reasons" *facts* which are indisputable? For that matter, are facts always—or ever—indisputable? It begins to look as though the proposed list of rules for behavior are not very important at all, but that what is important are the reasons being given for that behavior: not only whether or not they are convincing, but *why* they are or are not convincing. What makes a reason convincing? Whether or not a "reason" actually changes one's behavior is probably not a good criterion for something being a reason. There seem to be many good reasons for not smoking, acknowledged as such by the smoker, yet they do not lead (necessarily) to the cessation of smoking. Then should a course in ethics be expected to lead to one's acting morally? Probably not. If a moral theory were judged on its ability to inspire people to be moral, how would it differ from a pep talk, sermon, threat, or a psychoactive drug? It looks as though we must focus on the reasons given. Are these then subjective? Can one person's "reason" be another's "mere rhetoric?" Can ethics be supported by reason, and can reason, in turn, be supported in any way, or is it ultimately all subjective?

2. Abortion

For the sake of argument, we might begin by asking that we simply *assume* "the fetus is human." Then, if we can just agree on the exceptions, that is, on those circumstances wherein we agree that abortion would be justifiable, we might not have to settle the metaphysical question of when life begins. For example, would we agree that rape would justify an abortion? Would the fetus's threatening the life of the mother justify an abortion? Would the need for population control? Well, if we truly believed the fetus was a human being, perhaps nothing would justify taking its life. In a rape, the fetus is just an "innocent bystander"; in the case of threatening the mother's life, the fetus (if it is really human) has an equal claim to life, so perhaps we should flip a coin. It becomes evident that if we take seriously the assumption that the fetus is a human being, then no exceptions can be allowed, because we must give the fetus equal status with all other human beings. This will force us to reexamine the assumption that the fetus is a human (simply because the consequences of that assumption are now seen to be counterintuitive). So now we look at the biological/embryological data to see if there is a place we can draw a distinguishing line between "nonhuman being" and "human being." Quickening? Conception? Beginnings of heart beats or brain waves? Implantation? Viability? It would be ideal to find a real "gap" in nature (just as a teacher grading on a curve looks desperately for occasional "gaps" in the scattering of raw scores so that the labels A, B, and C seem more convincing). Short of a "natural gap," we might hope to find a place to draw the line which at least has some reasoning, some line of argument, that goes with it. As a last resort we could simply stipulate (i.e., arbitrarily) where the human/nonhuman line is to be drawn. But the more we move from that "natural gap" in reality to a stipulative definition, the more we worry. Why? Why is a definition so important? What is it to give "reasons" for this or that definition? Must those "reasons" represent an ideological base, or can we avoid that?

If nothing very convincing emerges from our flirtation with definitions, we must try a different tack. (Our method at this point will be questioned. It looks as though we are purposely trying to show that abortion is justifiable. Well, we are. So a discussion of this quasi-Popperian method is in order, along with some apt examples from medical science.) We might try this: we do kill human beings at times, or let them die. What are those circumstances, what are our reasons, and are they applicable to abortion? Might abortion really be considered a case of self-defense? (What are the crucial characteristics of self-defense that make it justifiable?) Or perhaps this is really a case of " not saving" as opposed to "killing" (that is, the pregnant woman is simply refusing to continue saving the fetus, she is not actually killing it). Do we find this distinction convincing in this set of circumstances? Is there a "natural role" or "duty" of a pregnant woman to save? What could this possibly mean; what could its foundation be?

In still another attempt, we might dig deeper by asking why we have moral rules against killing in the first place, and then wonder if those same reasons apply to the killing of fetuses. (This forces us into moral theory considerations a little prematurely. But it is a helpful initial glimpse and for our present purpose in the classroom we could stop short of a full discussion.)

Eventually we will see that there is a hard-core remainder who cannot tolerate killing of anything conceived by human beings, and who will be at loggerheads with some others. This is an excellent setting for some relevant issues to be explored: examining the claim of "sanctity of life," which will usually be the "principle" enunciated by the hard-core remainder; exploring why "loggerhead" issues are what they are and what the course and structure of a "normal" moral argument is (say, in appealing to more ultimate principles to which one's opponent agrees); investigating the role of emotions in moral arguments (e.g., why the showing of fetal photographs is considered unfair tactics by proabortionists).

Perhaps at this point it would be well to remind the reader what we are attempting here. An effort is being made to paraphrase several possible class discussions. No attempt is being made to discuss the relevant substantive issue, but rather only to show the kind of points and their sequence that usually surface in a course on medical ethics. The point is to give a more rooted, more realistic sense of what goes on in the classroom. Having this common exposure will help us considerably in focusing subsequent discussions, making comments more appropriate, abstractions more accurate, and strategies more easily understood. We will look at several more before stopping for comment.

3. Allocation

Not infrequently the neonatal intensive-care unit is filled to capacity. Requests to admit critical infants still come in. What considerations are relevant in deciding whether or not to remove an infant already there (resulting in its death) in order to make room for another? Ought quality of one's life count in allocating scarce resources, particularly when life itself is at stake? Transpose this to the adult world of renal dialysis. Could we bump someone from the machine if a "better" candidate came along? This would create an anxiety level in the adult situation not present in the neonate situation. Would that fact be a morally relevant difference between the two situations?

In the adult situation, what could "better candidate" mean? If "social" criteria are what is meant, then we must pursue the legitimacy of those particular values for deciding life and death matters. When life hangs in the balance, are a person's (or his parents' or his children's or his grandchildren's) contributions— potential, past, or current—relevant considerations? Do we hesitate because getting agreement on goods and their rankings is next to impossible, or because they are far too complicated to quantify accurately and reliably, or because they are irrelevant, or because if allocation were always so determined we would spend our lives in a state of nervous anxiety? Each of these lines must be followed out.

Many would quickly say that "social" criteria are irrelevant to a patient's selection (for, say, dialysis), but that *medical* criteria are clearly acceptable "factual" criteria for screening dialysis candidates. But why? Why should one's physical condition, mental condition, or possible longevity be relevant to selection for dialysis? The machine is putting in full time; it doesn't care if it is saving ten persons for one year each or one person for ten years. Why would we favor the one with a chance for longer life over several with shorter lives?

We have been focusing on a particular situation of allocation. We should enlarge the problem to health care in general, in order to see other conceptual connections of this issue. We must first of all be convinced that there are limits to resources, that we will forever be in a position of having much less than we could use. Then how do we divvy up the goodies? Equal shares? That can hardly make sense in medicine. Some need less, others more. How about by need? But all needs cannot be satisfied, so how can we determine which needs have priority? Could we establish norms, such that whoever falls beneath the norm may use enough resources to be brought up to the norm? That would imply that, e.g., the mentally retarded could be helped, but not the mentally gifted. Is that really fair? Do not the gifted also deserve to be helped? Pursue the concept of fairness; try to explicate it. So far in distribution we have appealed to "equal shares," "need," "merit," and "amounts necessary to bring up to a norm." Each of these, in certain contexts, seems to be the essence of fairness. But why? What is it about certain contexts that makes one or the other of these seem fair? And isn't it the case that where disputes remain it is because we disagree on which of these several senses of justice is appropriate for the context in question? Perhaps we should let the coin of the marketplace determine who gets what— if you can afford medical care or dialysis, or if you can purchase a new kidney or heart, then you "deserve" it. If one's society is capitalism, wouldn't this be moral? Isn't it the agreed-upon theory of government that makes certain things moral or not? Does what is right and fair for us derive solely from the form of government in which we find ourselves? Or are there criteria apart from government over against which we can measure the morality and justice of government? Would the utilitarian criteria be such? But aren't there many instances where utilitarian conclusions go counter to our intuitive sense of justice? How do we resolve this?

4. Paternalism

Solicit some examples of paternalism, and then begin closing in on what precisely makes those examples paternalistic. Can it be a value-free concept or does it necessarily imply that it is something we disapprove of? Is a person's pushing a child out of the way of a speeding car an act of paternalism? Why not? Must a person believe himself to have the expertise to help someone in order for his act to be considered paternalism? If the act is done for the good of that actor himself, can the act be considered paternalistic? If the client-patient thoroughly approves of the act "imposed" on him, is it appropriate to regard that act as paternalistic? Gradually the class evolves necessary and sufficient criteria for an act to be an instance of paternalism. Once they get the concept clear, the process of seeing when paternalism is justified and when it is not can be more explicitly and accurately attended to.

5. Moral Theory

It is ideal if one had held off explicit, head-on discussion of this issue until about two-thirds of the way or more through the course. Frequently, in the course of discussing other topics, ethical theory is touched upon or stumbled into. But still it is advantageous to back off. Keep a list of those issues to use when class pressure to deal explicitly with ethical theory has reached a peak. By waiting, sheer pent-up eagerness to tackle ethical theory in hopes of getting at some foundations will sustain a good and thorough discussion of these mildly esoteric issues. By having the students make so many claims and commitments on substantive issues thus far in the course, there will be considerable material to use in helping the students push back to the implicit foundations of their morality. Along with this clarification and subsequent critique, there are many related metaethical issues which are best worked over in this context. Precisely what *is* an ethical theory; how is it like a scientific theory, if at all? How is it distinct from a philosophy of life? Can it be proven or disproven? What does it take to discredit a moral theory? Can moral theories have much relevance if we all pretty much agree on what acts are right and wrong, yet have different theories to account for why those acts are right or wrong? Must moral theories have anything to do with motivation in order to be moral? What is the structure of a moral argument; how are clashes in basic moral principles resolved? What is the distinction between law, religion, and morality?

III. Second Order Reflections on the Paradigm

The strategy of the paradigm was to present a *particular* way of teaching ethics in a *particular* setting, namely, the medical school setting. It was meant to be a good example as well. This was to avoid those abstractions we quickly lapse into in talking about a variety of methods used in a variety of settings. Such abstractions are difficult for us to relate to, not having a clear sense of the particulars and the experiences from which they presumably arose. It was felt that developing a particular case in some detail would provide a more grounded, specifically understood point of departure for our subsequent contrasts, comparisons, and abstractions.

The paradigm now having been presented, we must stand back to consider somewhat more systematically what happened there. We will continue thinking in terms of teaching ethics in a medical school to students who are working toward their M.D. degree. This will provide the necessary focus before we briefly comment on other settings.

A. Class Discussion Commentary

The longest part of the paradigm was the attempt to give a précis, or an impressionistic sketch, of a few class sessions on several topics. Our point was not the pursuit of the substantive issue itself, but the focus and direction of class discussion. Inasmuch as references will be made to what went on there, it would be advisable to begin this "second-order reflection" with some observations about the focuses of classroom discussion.

Contrary to the view of many who have not experienced biomedical ethics classes firsthand, there is more going on than the simple recitation to each other of one's own pet principles and pithy moral sayings. It is not just a cataloging of who would say what—from Tom, Dick, and Mary (in the class) to Kant, Mill, and Rawls (not in the class). It is not a display of the standard observations and options on these standard issues, concluding with the standard question "well, what do you think"? Nor is it the instructor drilling and grilling the students into his own viewpoint.

Rather, there is a serious grappling with the issues, pushing everyone to move beyond his current thinking and to become aware of many other aspects and issues that bear on the one being considered by the class. The students are striving for clarity, a defensible position, and competence for dealing with such issues as they are confronted by them throughout life. For the most part they are forging their own way through ethics, with the helpful probing, direction, and occasional insights of a master teacher.

More specifically, with reference to the classroom paraphrases, good, analytic thinking in general was emphasized. There was a stress on ferreting out values that lie hidden, disguised as facts. There was much attention paid to getting clear on the facts, and seeing what role facts play (and do not play) in moral reasoning. Definitions per se were examined as to roles, kinds, dangers, and justifications. The structure of moral arguments was studied: their process, foundations, strategies, limitations, deadlocks, and conceptual geography. Key concepts were explicated (as in the paternalism session). Such explication is of crucial importance in doing ethics. Epistemological questions arose, as did metaphysical ones. Concepts of reason, person, self, freedom, and emotion had to be dealt with, if only to see precisely how they were relevant. The possible roles, foundations, and "testing" of ethical theories were worked over. Helpful analogies and disanalogies with scientific theories were explored. The "ecology" of moral concerns was displayed and pursued, showing, for example, the interrelatedness of individual morality to matters of justice to the system of government. In short, students were being trained in broad analytical and critical skills in the course of their becoming informed and sensitive to moral issues directly relevant to their profession.

B. Goals

Goals are tricky. One never knows how general or how specific to make them. Should they be ultimate ("enrich life"), or proximate ("instill a sense of the evolving of history and its influences on us"), or immediate ("know the names of the generals on both sides in the Civil War")?

Stated goals can of course be self-serving. The author has seen many course syllabi which meticulously state goals for each section of the course, and they are exactly synonomous with each topic. [Goal: to know the three causes of child abuse. Topic: The three causes of child abuse]. In other words, the goal is to learn exactly what it is that is being taught. It is not clear which came first.

In considering the goals of teaching ethics in a medical school, more is at stake than advertising a course, satisfying the Educational Resources Department, or keeping the instructor honest. The goals are usually fashioned with "justification" in mind. This is inevitable in a curriculum already packed like a plenum and with a multitude of new topics (and endless elaboration of old topics) waiting in the wings for inclusion center stage. So goals as discussed here have that practical imperative of justification as a backdrop.

It is not the purpose here to argue out competing claims, as a curriculum committee might do. Rather our focus is on what the teaching of ethics can contribute to the end product of medical school teaching, namely, the physician—as person, as professional, as policymaker.

The Report of The Hastings Center Project, *The Teaching of Ethics in Higher Education,* articulated several goals which are helpful and important wherever ethics is taught. The Report elaborates five goals: (1) stimulating the moral imagination, (2) recognizing ethical issues, (3) developing analytical skills, (4) eliciting a sense of moral obligation and personal responsibility, and (5) tolerating and resisting disagreement and ambiguity.[4] What is discussed below concerning goals will be in complete accord with that Report, and indeed will be an elaboration of those goals. However the discussion here will be fashioned more specifically to the medical school context.

1. General Goals

We will begin by looking at some of the more broadly conceived goals, that is, goals an ethics teacher might well want to accomplish in a medical school setting, but which in fact might also be accomplished by teaching a subject other than ethics. Recall the description of the context as a "conceptual ghetto" as discussed above. Given that, an important goal is to shift the focus, to break out of the prevailing narrow mind-set, to set before these students a new set of concerns and a new method for dealing with them.

Part of this general goal is to break down that commonly held belief, "science is hard-core, all else is soft." It is an important move toward maturation to discover where in fact parts of science are soft and parts of nonscience are hard. Students can be led to experience rigorous thinking in ethics courses. Besides being a startling revelation, it is immensely gratifying to them. That in itself is another general goal; it has something to do with self-image. It is important to their personal growth to develop skills that help clarify, organize, and articulate aspects of that great inchoate mass of nonscience that surrounds them and affects their lives, but which had seemed impenetrable to reason. It is as though some inroads into it, however small, give a sense of control as well as fascination with that which had seemed intuitively significant, but mushy and mysterious beyond manageability.

Another general goal is to develop a sense of how tightly entwined facts and values are, how one must constantly be alert to the possibility of values "disguised" as facts, and how one might go about unraveling them. These are not necessarily *moral* values, but wherever there are values of any sort around (especially if hidden), a moral issue involving them cannot be far away. The prevalence of such hidden values in the medical world in everything from diagnosis to laboratory values makes this goal all the more important.

A general goal of some importance in this context is teaching students how to disagree without acrimony, indeed, teaching them how to use disagreement creatively to forge new awareness, sounder principles, tighter arguments, and increased understanding. As described in the paradigm, these persons have for the most part had little opportunity for the give and take of meaningful discussion. They have been too busy recording "facts." And inasmuch as this also implies they have been dealing in disciplines that primarily have facts to be recorded, there is a general goal that is a corollary to the one just mentioned: to give the students practice in tolerance, a lesson best taught when dealing with matters having a degree of inherent ambiguity, such as ethics. Some of the most vital aspects of our lives, particularly those that give our lives meaning, manifest this qualitiy of ambiguity. ("Ambiguity" is not the term one would, on analysis, choose to use for this referred-to quality, but for the moment it will do.) One learns that there are gaps that cannot—or not yet— be filled in, assumptions that cannot be proved (or disproved), concepts that are variously understood, variables too difficult and multitudinous to control, and data too ambiguous for interpretation. One learns that the world is far more complicated than one thought, that equally rational people can disagree, and that tolerance for each other and for unresolved ambiguity is a means of survival and a route to discovery.

2. Ethics' specific goals

The central and usual argument concerning the teaching of ethics courses pivots around the question, "Will an ethics course make the students more moral?" The usual answer is, "No, not necessarily." Just as sheer medical knowledge does not necessarily motivate students to go out and use it for doing good, so knowledge of ethical theory and moral arguments does not necessarily motivate students to go forth and be moral. Or, so it seems. But of course the matter is more complicated than any of these comments would suggest. Certainly if the students were motivated to be moral in the first place, they would become "morally better" simply by virtue of now making better moral judgments. In morally complicated situations they are now better equipped to work their way through to a better (i.e., morally justifiable) solution. Here teaching has helped their acumen, but not necessarily their motivation. Comparing the teaching of ethics to sex education in high school is in all respects more apt.

But there is more to an ethics course than learning one's way around in a moral argument. One's sensitivity to morally relevant facts is heightened; one sees moral issues where before one had seen none. (This is not an idle mission. One of the most surprising phenomena about students and professionals is their inability to recognize moral problems as such.) Being exposed to moral arguments stretches one's imagination—"see it from the other's point of view," "put yourself in his place," see it as an "ideal observer," "universalize the principle on which you are acting," imagine yourself "behind the veil of ignorance." With such focus, emphasis, and highlighting one could hardly miss being— at least for awhile—hypersensitive to the feelings and thoughts of others, and to the moral aspects of situations. One's perception may become more accurate; his judgments more sound.

One of the goals is to convey a seriousness of purpose, to convey that these matters are of the utmost importance. Even the fact that curriculum time is designated is a strong message in a medical school. But somehow the teacher must do more. He or she must transmit the message that this enterprise is not just a mind game, but deals with matters of profound significance to self, society, and profession.

There remains to mention as a goal the development of analytical skills in moral matters. Of course, in everything that has been said here about goals, analytical skills have been presumed. Courses in ethics focus on arguments and lines of reasoning. Concepts are explicated as necessary; foundations and assumptions are uncovered and examined. One gets involved in specific moral issues, then one stands back to reflect on the reasoning apparatus itself (assumptions, concepts, strategies, lines of reasoning). This is all done in a language and manner understandable to medical students; indeed, it is primarily they who initiate these second-level, philosophical reflections and who work through the issues in discussion, under the guidance of the teacher.

Perhaps it should be mentioned that several things are specifically *not* goals: (1) indoctrination into a particular position on a
particular issue; (2) turning the medical students into philosophers, as though they were getting a "straight" course in philosophy rather than being helped to see and understand some of their
professional problems from a philosophical perspective; (3) having the students learn and remember all the details, pro and con,
on all the major moral issues of their profession instead of having
them develop the knack of rigorously pursuing such issues on
their own; (4) presenting a philosophy of life, replete with recom-
mended values and ways of living.

C. Methods and Formats

We are still focusing on the medical school setting; we are
simply standing back from the model presented to discuss what
was shown there and to look more broadly at some alternatives.
The paradigm and the standback reflections on it are our way of
keeping a Pandora's box contained and orderly.

In discussing various aspects and methods of teaching ethics to
medical students, it would be helpful to organize these comments
around several settings: (1) the classroom, (2) the clinic, (3) other
formats.

1. The classroom

The most crucial factor, in the view of the author, is that
classes be conducted in small groups of approximately fifteen
students. Not only does this change from medical school standard
format appear as warm and welcome to the students, but it seems
the best (perhaps only) way of accomplishing the goals described
in the last section. This method actively engages students in
working through problems, in thinking along with the others and
the teacher. They are not learning material by rote; they are *using*
it. They struggle to articulate; they try out ideas, reject them,
revise them, and try again. There is immediate feedback. This
give-and-take of discussion (rather than didactic lecture) further
enhances the message that accumulation of more information is
not the point, but rather how one deals with the information one
already has.

For somewhat similar reasons, it is important to have the same teacher(s) throughout the course. Continuity, building on previous points, pushing each student farther in his or her own thinking can mostly be done only if the teacher is aware of what has gone before and what will probably come up later. This is not in opposition to having an occasional guest teacher (along with the regular teacher); in fact an occasional guest is usually appreciated by the students, often beyond the guest's actual contribution. What it is opposed to is the course's being a parade of guest lecturers.

Team-teaching is a different matter. In that case, presumably, the teachers are always there together. It is not clear what the advantage is, unless the ethical problem deals with an area so factually complicated that the presence of a knowledgeable person in that area is necessary to be sure that problems as they are posed, reasoned about, and resolved are in accurate accord with the facts. A rather common danger of team-teaching of this sort is that it all too clearly embodies and perpetuates the "two cultures" ideology. Worse, there is an inevitable sense of equal time, so that far more details of the facts are elaborated and lectured about than necessary. Valuable time and momentum for in-depth pursuit of ethical issues are thus lost. (This approach makes more sense in an undergraduate, graduate, or nonscience professional school setting, where this "study" of science is as liberating and enlarging as "ethics" can be in a medical setting.)

Some team-teaching makes more sense in the medical setting. Some of the science courses that deal with sensitive areas (say, genetics or reproductive biology) may invite a teacher of ethics to make a presentation or two dealing with the ethically sensitive parts of the field. This is no substitute for a medical ethics course, but it is a good supplement and reinforcement to a basic medical ethics course.

There are those who would argue that professional ethics should always be taught in the midst of the regular professional courses. Otherwise, it is argued, the ethical considerations will not bear on professional interests, but rather be isolated and insulated into their own courses, and then forgotten—or at least conveniently overlooked. Again, the ideal is to have it both ways: the ethics course in addition to the integration. However, if it had to be one way or the other, this author would opt for the individual course devoted to ethics, especially in the medical school.

In the integrated course, ethics does not get nearly the time it needs to do the job necessary (as delineated under "goals," above). At best it brings the issues to a conscious level. But at worst, it suffers by comparison with the rest of the course, which has the interest, time, and momentum to involve the student. There ethics comes along, if not as an afterthought, as a weak second, and does not have time to immerse the students in the rigors, skills, and excitement of ethics. Ethics runs the risk of losing ground rather than gaining. It takes a course of its own to capture the student's imagination, involvement, and interest. Far better is it for students who have honed their moral perceptions and analytic skills in the dialectic of an ethics seminar to be sent out into their other professional courses to raise questions and pursue moral issues. (Of course, it is still better to have a critical mass of humanistic disciplines, each being taught in its exclusive course, so that these perspectives on life and medicine subsequently reach and influence the entire medical center community, legitimizing such concerns and interests by their very presence.)

The variety of moral issues of interest and importance to the medical students is too well known to review here, (see section V-C, below), but some generalities about their arrangement might be in order. Medical students by sheer orientation and perhaps self-selection are problem-oriented. It is well to capitalize on this. For all their announced reluctance "to philosophize," once they get caught up in a problem, they are off and running! This author follows a general rule with these students: "never do philosophy until forced to by the students." If the teacher starts with philosophical frameworks, theories, distinctions, and so on, the students will find them unreal and irrelevant. If instead the teacher gets the students hooked on a puzzle or a problem (a real one, to be sure), the students in their fervor and commitment to solving the problem will begin to do philosophy on their own. That is, they will raise the epistemological concerns and positions, analyze assumptions, make crucial distinctions, and so on. They can do excellent work, and the teacher's role is to fan the flames: sharpening points, clarifying, and giving occasional mini-lectures to unravel a difficult conceptual entanglement they have gotten into. Once the students have seen a problem they will go to great lengths to solve it—indulging in philosophy, distinctions, hypotheticals, theories, or whatever else they think might help.

Closely related to this point is a strategy for dealing explicitly with ethical theory in these courses. Many teachers believe that no real discussion of ethical issues can take place unless a few weeks in the beginning are devoted to ethical theory, history of ethics, and "what is ethics?" This seems a particularly deadly way to begin, and probably unproductive. If it arouses interest at all, it gives rise to abstract and sophomoric debates as to whether or not ethics is possible, and whether morality can be anything beyond mere emotivism. Far better is it to get the students involved, for at least half a term, working through actual moral problems, making points and counterpoints, refuting, accepting, and discarding positions. By then two significant things have happened: (1) Considerable pressure has built up to deal with the more abstract matter of ethical theory and its foundations. The students have come to see it as very important and are anxious for some clarity and organization of those issues. Each issue discussed up to this point, in being pushed to the limits, has generated some questions and lines of reasoning that are most helpfully dealt with in this segment of the course. (2) Easy, simplistic dismissals of moral reasoning are no longer possible, for the students themselves have been enthusiastically engaged in arguing moral issues for at least five or six weeks. They have, in a sense, committed themselves, and are now in a better position to try to understand that commitment. It is not as hypothetical and abstract as it would have been had these same questions of ethical theory come up in the beginning weeks.

Other than the placement of the ethical theory discussion, it is not clear that one sequence of problems is better than another. What is important is that there be a rationale for the arrangement. That is, the sequence of discussed problems should be such that general themes, points, and strategies come up that can be built on and enlarged in a subsequent problem. This not only reinforces the learning and conveys a sense of increasing and cumulative abilities, but it counteracts the tendency to think of these issues as isolated anecdotes, totally situational, and without connecting similarities.

This emphasis on having the course be problem-oriented does not necessarily mean case studies. The "problem" of "problem-orientation" is more general than a case study, referring to such as abortion, euthanasia, allocation, truth-telling, confidentiality, and so on. Case studies are apt to entice students into so much wallowing in particularities that they lose track of the relevant conceptual framework and principles. Needless to say, it is possible to begin with a case study, and then gradually widen and vary the parameters. With some topics and some cases it can be a felicitous beginning to a problem area. However, generally, case studies as starters bog down in irrelevancies and misfocus attention. They seem to be more effective when brought in to sharpen the issues (after a more general discussion) and to test out some of the conclusions derived from the more general discussion. Often it is such use of a case that will make clear to the students that they have to go back to the drawing board on an issue they thought they had resolved.

The various techniques that can be used in a classroom will not be discussed here. This varies greatly with a teacher's interests and skills, and the medical school setting does not seem to rule out any in particular. There does always seem (in the medical setting) to be a penchant toward realism, which (at least initially) seems to make film dramatizations or role playing less effective. A real patient describing a situation or problem would have more effect. The students are simply oriented that way—toward an individual person and his or her problem. (Medical students always seem to learn faster, deeper, and longer the biomedical aspects of a disease existing in a patient whom they know.) Seldom does such a gimmick add to the actual discussion or insights, but it tends to make it more memorable and interesting to the students.

This writer tends to use none of these devices at all. He finds no satisfactory substitute for steady, rigorous, head-to-head seminar discussion, with the teacher keeping the discussion focused, clear, relevant, advancing, and challenging. Films tend to give a scattering of opinions without depth (except for some films that present a problem filmed in "real life," like the now-famous burn victim film *Please Let Me Die).* Classroom debates, which some teachers use, are not as satisfactory as our seminar dialogue. The former seems to degenerate into "debater's points" and winning;

the latter seems to function more as a joint search for truth.

There seems to be no clear guidance on the matter of examinations and papers. However, an interesting way of thinking about the matter is in terms of the self-image of the teacher. He or she often feels strongly that this course must be taken as seriously and get as much respect as any course in the medical school, and that the way to guarantee this is to give exams, thus letting the students know the course is tough and important. (The reader can fill in all the other trappings usually accompanying this "equal importance" emphasis.) The effectiveness (or its lack) of this approach very likely depends upon local circumstances and the personality of the teacher.

This author has seen the matter rather differently. Observing the pressures, schedules, and goals in a medical school, he found it very effective *not* to compete as Herr Professor cracking the whip, but almost as a colleague of the students prepared to work alongside them on the difficult moral problems facing the medical world. Elsewhere the students felt they were being judged and examined at every turn. It seemed appropriate (given the collegial imagery just suggested) not to add to the paranoia and examination stress. The disadvantages of giving exams seemed to outweigh the gains.

Similarly, writing and reading assignments might well take seriously the context of the medical school. "Think papers" (short, but frequent papers working on a limited problem confronted in class, reading, or discussion) do this nicely. Writing such papers gives the students the satisfaction of having reasoned through a problem without the burden of having to produce a lengthy, finely finished paper. Again, in this context of busyness and information overload, ethics can probably be taught more effectively by bringing in as little new information as possible, by dealing with as few details and minutiae as possible, and by helping to clarify and organize the morass of details the students have already accumulated. The many facts and details of argument around these moral issues will quickly be forgotten. Our job is to equip the students for the longer run: sharpened perceptions on moral issues, a sense of how to approach and pursue a moral problem, a clear and critical grasp of ethical reasoning and its foundations, and of its pivotal strengths and weaknesses.

This same emphasis is true for reading assignments. They should be chosen carefully so as to avoid wordiness, jargon, conceptual clutter, meandering lines of reason, and the elaboration of philosophical niceties. Often the appropriate readings are not those wherein philosophers are writing for other philosophers. Good choices are rather those articles usually appearing in medical or scientific journals and written for the lay person. These can be provocative, clear, and competent. If more philosophy needs to be done, it can be done in the classroom, with the teacher gently leading the way. It is also useful to put on reserve optional readings that are in fact more philosophical and more substantive. The students are usually on differing levels of experience and maturity in the humanistic disciplines, and this can be partially overcome by having optional readings available for the more advanced students to replace their assigned reading.

2. The clinical setting

Often the teaching of medical ethics takes place in a clinical setting. This is an effective setting for such teaching. As we have said, having the patient and the problem immediately before one makes the ethical issue dramatic and memorable. There is an urgency that the classroom does not have. That, however, is not all to the good. Without the standback time to reflect, to play around with the issue by trying a variety of approaches and by hypothesizing different variables, it is a lesser learning experience, which does not enlarge one's understanding in dealing with future cases. The urgency draws our attention to this single case in all its particularity. Analogous to a straightforward medical problem, there is very little time. A decision must be made, and the next patient seen. This is apt to turn into a service function rather than a teaching function. That is, the ethics teacher is perhaps being consulted for the immediate problem, but not being given a chance to convert it into a teaching situation. This is not to say teaching cannot be done in the clinical setting; it is, in fact, done. It is only to point to some inadequacies and dangers. These drawbacks can be partially overcome by setting aside a later time to discuss one or another of the cases in more detail, thus transforming a service function into a genuine teaching situation.

Assuming that this clinical setting is in a teaching hospital, there are some additional benefits. One is that faculty, residents, and students are involved, so that the teaching reaches and is contributed to by a much wider spectrum than is found in the usual classroom. Also, the very presence of the ethics teacher has an interesting effect on the others. It is like a visual reminder of certain aspects of health care that might otherwise be overlooked. Everyone develops more attentiveness to the moral aspects, as though the presence of this "specialist" legitimates focus and attention on those aspects which are his or her specialty. And lastly, this setting focuses more directly on the everyday moral problems faced by physicians, instead of on the more global and exotic ones that tend to be discussed in the classroom.

This writer prefers "attending rounds" to "work rounds" for clinical teaching. Work rounds involve the medical team's flurry of activity, going in and out of patients' rooms to decide and prescribe. The clinical imperative (to get the work done) is at its greatest. Attending rounds take place removed from the immediate presence of the patients and are more like chart reviews. There is more time for questioning and general hypothesizing. Attending rounds are more dialectical and relaxed. The clinical imperative is clearly present here as well, but is not quite as overwhelming. It is good teaching time.

This raises an issue which should be mentioned here, but without elaboration. It is that there is a strong difference of opinion on whether or not the ethics teacher should see patients with the physician, particularly in the outpatient clinic. Is this an intrusion on a special, protected, traditional relationship of intimacy between doctor and patient? Yet how can the ethics teacher be attuned to the nuances and subtleties apart from this actual involvement? Oddly enough, in this writer's experience, it is the physicians who are urging the involvement and the teachers who are shying away from the intrusion.

3. Other Forums

There are many possible settings for teaching that would more accurately be regarded as supplementary. These are too sporadic to give the continuity and depth needed for real teaching, but consciousness raising and transmission of information can and do take place, and in an important way. These discussions, occurring as they do in public forums, underscore the importance of moral concerns and in addition reach staff, faculty, and residents, as well as students.

(i) "Grand rounds" is usually a formal, weekly presentation of a timely medical topic. Often each "service" (medicine, surgery, obstetrics-gynecology, psychiatry, and so on) has its own grand rounds. Within this format moral concerns can on occasion be presented and discussed. It is a good opportunity because there is real integration of the clinical data with the moral issue. Whether or not "medical ethics" or "medical humanities" should have its *own* regular grand rounds is a question best answered in light of local factors: the size of the medical center, its geographical spread, the breadth of support within the medical community, the size of the humanities staff.

One suspects the burden of proof should be on those who want to have their own regular grand rounds for ethics. It can indeed work well. Yet there must be special circumstances to recommend that approach, because there is obviously so much to be said for ethics being integrated into the ongoing discussion formats of medicine. Ethics should not be seen as isolated or as a subspecialty, but rather as an ingredient concern throughout medicine. One hates to ghettoize it unless there are special circumstances that recommend such a move.

(ii) Situational teaching is not a standard format, but it is both a service and teaching function the ethics teacher could offer. Not infrequently moral problems arise around a patient in the hospital, causing considerable confusion, tension, and division among the staff. Those are ideal times for an impromptu "seminar" with the staff and whatever students and physicians are currently on that service. This has all the motivation and attention of urgency with sufficient time to do some in-depth analysis. It is obviously a teaching situation, but it is also a service, inasmuch as it helps heal staff division and often assists in making a decision on the case.

Two observations are relevant at this point concerning grand rounds, situational teaching, and clinical involvement in general. Particularly for situational teaching, a considerable amount of trust and respect must have developed between the staff and the ethics teacher. The staff is not likely to bring an "outsider" into the inner workings and worries of their service. And there are already plenty of moral points of view being expressed over any given issue. So the teacher must not only be seen as a trusted insider, but as one who can bring some clarity and insight to the situation. The criteria for trust is not difficult: simply being low-key, pleasant, reasonable, and a familiar face in its part of the hospital might suffice.

The other observation is that teachers from the humanistic disciplines are likely to overprepare for presentations. That in itself is not bad, of course. But when the perceived need to prepare so extensively leads them to turn down invitations to present and comment, then it is unfortunate. The teaching hospital community operates very differently. Staff and physicians are generally working so all out that they are accustomed to doing presentations (at least of a relatively informal sort) without much preparation at all. Elaborate preparation simply cannot be expected from them, and most can talk spontaneously from experience, or from a recent case. There is such a wealth of experience and such an infinite amount to learn that this informal system of teaching and learning seems thoroughly appropriate. It is a system the ethics teacher could slip into to some advantage. It might offend his or her sense of thoroughness, detail, and depth, but nevertheless, as a supplemental endeavor, it is worth it. It is indeed piecemeal, but it is a format the medical community is familiar with, along with its shortcomings and dangers.

(iii) A very effective way of reaching faculty and staff is by means of an off-campus "retreat." It is ideal if it can be out of beeper range but within emergency distance time. One day or a day and a half (overnight) is about the right length of time. About twenty persons is a good size. A fairly well-delineated topic should be planned, and two or three relevant readings sent out in advance. In this writer's experience these retreats have been enthusiastically received and immensely successful. Along with the excellence of discussion and the chance to pursue issues in relaxed, congenial circumstances is the rapport and trust that is significantly enhanced, not just between "humanist" and clinician, but among the clinicians as well. It is an opportunity to discuss in depth with their colleagues issues of deep concern that are seldom addressed in the normal working day.

Of course this retreat can be worked out in a variety of ways for a variety of personnel and students. Those possible permutations need not be elaborated here. It is important to mention it in that, in view of the extreme busyness and hustle of a medical center, a retreat setting is especially valuable for the study of moral issues.

(iv) The Continuing Education Program for physicians, which exists in most medical schools, may offer an opportunity for teaching ethics. This could vary from a two-hour session to a week's workshop. There is by no means a teeming mass of practicing physicians out there desirous of thinking about ethical problems in medicine. Indeed, an ethics teacher whose experience is limited to an academic medical center will be mildly shocked at the lack and level of interest among practicing physicians. This is largely because of a misunderstanding of what ethics is all about, and of their having had their medical education at a time when these matters were not drawing much attention. However, they do come with their own set of moral dilemmas in daily practice that are different from the standard. (Is it immoral for me to reject Medicaid patients, when, if I accept *any*, they will *all* come to me and I can't make a living at what I am paid for treating them? Is it morally all right for me to give medication or an injection to a patient who does not really need it, since if I don't, she or he will go to another physician down the street, and I will have lost a patient? I can't afford to lose more patients. Is it immoral of me to sell my practice when I move or retire?) It is, in any case, a ripe field for a pioneer teacher. The issues raised in the course of daily practice may be as much in the realm of "business ethics" as medical ethics.

D. Attitudes, Obstacles, and Evaluation

For the most part these matters are not much different at a medical school from those at other institutions of learning. A few might be emphasized, but elaboration is not necessary.

(i) Students, as was pointed out earlier, are anxious to be medical professionals. They are nervous and insecure with their medical knowledge and their professional identity. Boy Scouts are better with first aid; lab technicians with procedures. Thus, that which looks like a continuation of college is not on the surface appealing to them. Also, they tend to have the view (discussed earlier) of hard-core medicine vs. soft, mushy non-medicine. The latter, they figure, is something anyone can manage with a bit of slickness and rhetoric. Additionally, the curriculum is tightly filled from boundary to boundary.

The only solution for this is excellent teaching. If one is challenging and stimulating minds at the highest levels, is clearly not wasting time, and is bringing important clarification which is obviously helpful, then obstacles and attitudes are overcome. Formats, supportive clinicians, and friendly curriculum committees are minor compared to effective teaching. It can lead to dramatic reversals of obstructive attitudes.

Of course, if one cannot even get a foot in the door, there is no chance to succeed at teaching. But medical ethics courses have started in a variety of ways, often student-initiated (more so, no doubt, in the early seventies). Some new colleges of medicine have instituted such courses from the start. Often medical science faculty or clinicians have started the courses, eventually inviting in more traditionally trained ethics teachers to help or to take over. The course can also grow out of a small interested discussion group within the school, or result from a symposium or workshop held at the school.

(ii) The two leading obstacles to developing ethics courses are (1) the crowded curriculum, and (2) misunderstanding of what ethics is all about. There is no end to the further knowledge we think a physician should have. The case must be made for ethics (and other humanistic disciplines in a medical school) that it is not just more of the same, not just further filigree on what is already given, but instead meets a more basic personal, social, and epistemological need, which in some sense might be extremely important to "holding all the rest of it together." (That metaphor will not be unpacked here.) Its goal is to integrate, not simply to add more information.[5]

There is an additional problem created by the crowded curriculum. That has to do with finding times to meet in a small seminar, rather than being put in a single time slot and thus having to deliver lectures to a large group. Indeed, it would be well to meet in small groups at any odd hours of the day or night to avoid this. Surely successful lectures are possible, and there are other techniques, such as designating a different group of fifteen students every "lecture" hour, with whom the teacher discusses while all the others become observers. However, small discussion sections are more apt to achieve the goals.

Whether or not the course is elective or required must be determined by local factors, such as what is done with other, similar courses. An ideal arrangement is to make it a "selective" instead of an "elective." That is, if other courses are given (say, other humanistic discipline courses) that meet the same general goals (see above III-B), then it may be required that some courses be taken, but no specific course. This capitalizes on the student's initial interest, that is, he can choose the course he wants.

One might imagine that requiring a course turns the students against it. That is not altogether true. How well the course is taught is far more important. Requirement is just as apt to please the students by giving them the courage of their convictions. That is, they might very well like to take the course, but if it is an elective, they are afraid to take it lest meanwhile their fellow students who do not take it get ahead of them in the "medically relevant" subjects. Thus they are relieved if it is a required course, for they can then take it without being penalized.

The obstacle presented by the misunderstanding of ethics occurs frequently. The suspicion that ethics teachers are reformers who will be snooping, propagating slogans, drawing up regulations, and generally interfering with the physician's style and decisionmaking is pervasive. Underlying this is the common belief that ethics is totally subjective, just a matter of one person's tastes. Therefore, its opponents would argue, who is any one person to impose his tastes onto an enterprise of which that person is not even a part, who is unfamiliar with the nuances and subtleties of the practice of medicine? There is no way around this obstacle short of a slow, steady process of proving otherwise, of actually being a help and building trust. As has been continually emphasized, excellence in teaching is the cornerstone to success.

(iii) Evaluation is an immensely difficult matter. The major discussion concerning ethics teaching in medical schools always centers on "will it make a difference in their behavior, and can it be measured." As indicated in the Report of The Hastings Center Project on the Teaching of Ethics, if teaching ethics is meant to change behavior, it does so only in a subtle way.[6] One does expect that students will become more morally perceptive and make better decisions on morally problematic situations. One difficulty is that we do not require this kind of justification for microbiology, gross anatomy, histology, and other medical sciences. And to a practicing physician, it is not at all obvious that many of those medical science fields actually help them make decisions. At least, they might say, their helpfulness is in no way commensurate with the hours spent studying the fields. Given that there is no clear way to justify the various traditional medical studies, or the particular number of hours spent in them, it is odd therefore to require it of ethics which seems to be as intuitively justified by need and use as the other fields. Even if the effects of the ethics course were measured, what would one compare the results to? It might show that it made a difference, but is it enough of a difference to make room for it in the curriculum? Since there are no similar statistics for the other courses, there is no basis for such a curricular decision.

One also would have to question any result because the information being measured is so diluted by time variables. What is being suggested is that the effects of *one* course be measured; that is, *one* course out of four *years* of courses and some three to five years of subsequent on-the-job training. Perhaps if a total program in human values (say, a Department of Humanities within the medical school) were being evaluated in terms of subsequent effect, the measurements might be somewhat more believable.

An evaluation too simple and mundane to be of interest to the statistician, but of tremendous help to the teacher of the course, is the evaluation form filled out by the student at the conclusion of the course. This should be done each time the course is given. How the course is helping the student right now in discerning moral issues, reasoning through them, and generally knowing what's what in ethical theories and argumentation is at least as important as its effect on the student's behavior ten years from now! And in any case, it would be a pity to allow evaluation to become the tail that wags the dog. Many intuitively important and exciting projects have been abandoned because there was no way of measuring results. And conversely, many simple-minded projects have been approved and funded primarily because there was a clear and decisive instrument for evaluating results.

A valuable means of evaluation is the site-visit review team. Some years it could be a team made up of persons from within the institution; and at other times from outside the institution. This team would study syllabi, interview faculty, students, staff, and generally prowl into any areas and by any means it thought helpful and appropriate (and moral). It would then submit a report concerning strengths, weaknesses, and recommendations. This endeavor is more appropriate for evaluating a program rather than a single course, but variations of it could easily relate to the special needs of a particular institution. The reports of these site-visit teams could also be very helpful in dealing with granting agencies, deans, and curriculum committees.

E. Teachers and Credentials

This topic, like many others dealt with here, is so full of variables one is reluctant to make any general statements. Again we must be content with some general observations that one might take into consideration in deciding on the particulars of one's own situation. It will be assumed that we are talking about training for teachers in the substantive areas of bioethics, and not in methods of teaching. This is not to suggest that the skills of teaching are unimportant (we have continually stressed the importance of good teaching) but only that they are no different for teaching in a medical school setting than for teaching in any other setting.

This issue of "certification" of the teacher usually takes shape around two focuses, as discussed in the Report of The Hastings Center Project on the Teaching of Ethics:[7] (1) Should the teacher be a person primarily in the field of medicine or in the field of ethics? (2) If any training in ethics is necessary, should it be a religious or a philosophical training?

Obviously the goals have much to do with deciding this matter one way or another. If mere raising of consciousness is all that is desired, then any person well read in the field can do it. That is, anyone who can read can probably see and roughly understand the gathering of points on each side of a moral issue in bio-medicine. Systematically displaying these respective accumulations to students will suffice for raising consciousness.

An analogous situation exists in the clinical setting. If our goal is primarily to influence and motivate the student's behavior, then a morally sensitive physician who can become a model for the student would be very effective.

If, however, the goals, instead of or in conjunction with those just mentioned, are to sharpen the student's skills at moral reflection, to gain clarity on lines of reasoning and ethical foundations, and to attempt to pursue and resolve the student's doubts, questions, and blind commitments, then it seems evident that the teacher must have a good training in ethical theory. It takes considerable skill and experience on the part of a teacher to detect the key words and strategies of each student so as to pick up on pivotal points, leading the student to a line of questioning through which he or she might come upon new discoveries and enlarged perspectives. Whether it is a point of epistemology, or logic, or metaphysics, or esthetics, or whatever, the teacher must be familiar with that terrain, sensing its role in the student's thinking, where it leads, and how to deal with it. (Observe the paradigm, II-C above, of a classroom flow of ideas on sample issues. Note their range and general tenor.)

Whether this training in ethics comes by way of religion or philosophy probably does not matter. Each has its strengths. The philosopher tends to deal with ethics as independently as possible of various ideologies. The religious studies teacher should be able to draw out and explore the religious foundations of various moral positions, and conversely to see their implications. Inasmuch as many students are religious, and anticipate having patients who are also, exploring ethics within the religious context could be very helpful.

The philosophically trained ethics teacher would be searching for ethical foundations independent of religion, or of any metaphysical beliefs (if possible). Since morality should be relevant for all persons, this teacher would try to deal with the more universal aspects of morality, though trying to show where religious beliefs fit in—or do not fit in—to this more universal scheme.

In point of fact, however (and more's the pity) there is probably very little difference between how a religious studies teacher and a philosopher teach biomedical ethics. The points and the arguments as they generally occur in a classroom over the various topics, all look pretty much alike. The pity is that this probably indicates a contentment with simply raising consciousness rather than with deeper probing into epistemological points and metaphysical foundations.

In summary of these particular points, we might say: (i) For maximum motivation and minimum understanding, train medically with a morally sensitive physician; (ii) for minimum motivation and maximum understanding of the "deeper structures" of ethical theory, go to the classroom of one trained specifically in ethics. (The chief difference between those trained in religious ethics and those trained in philosophical ethics will probably be the approach, description, and logic of those "deep structures"); and (iii) for consciousness raising alone, *simpliciter,* go to anyone available who is well read on the discussions of the various topics of bioethics.

However, how nice to have some of everything! As we have stressed throughout, a single course in ethics is much too limited an effort. There ought to be places where consciousness is raised, other places where one sees at firsthand ideal moral behavior, and still other settings where a formal attempt is made to understand ethics. Reinforcement of these learning situations should reverberate throughout the academic medical center, each reinforcing and enlarging on the other.

The most important additional requirement of one already trained in ethics is great familiarity with the medical and medical educational world. This cannot be stressed enough. It goes without saying that it is essential to have detailed factual knowledge of those medical areas concerning which one is raising moral questions. But that is not what is being emphasized here. Rather the emphasis is on familiarity with the "atmosphere," the ambience, of medicine and medical education. Usually these matters do not seem substantively relevant, yet somehow they affect the teacher's acceptance, believability, and ability to communicate at an important level with the students and staff. Such familiarity seems to consist of knowing the interests, the compulsions, the peeves, the purposes, the styles, the experiences, and the fears generally pervasive throughout the medical school and hospital. One who is not sensitive to these matters comes off as somehow inappropriate and unreal. At best he or she is regarded as irrelevant; at worst as incompetent. This emphasis on having assimilated the nuances of the ambience is of course this writer's interpretation; one doubts that even students would know exactly why they were or were not taking this or that teacher seriously.

What a philosopher or a literature professor could get a class in a liberal arts college or graduate school excited about is very different from that which would excite a medical student. It is as though a shift has taken place in the mind-set of a medical student—brought about by different pressures, immediate aims, time limitations, hopes and fears. No time now for the professor's wild but fascinating tangent, sparked by an incidental comment in class; impatience now with the elaborate fabricated hypothetical situation of the philosopher in an effort to make a point. A teacher *can* get medical students back into those other frames of mind, but only by starting out being highly sensitive to and in accord with medical students' mind-set and atmosphere, and then gently building a bridge from that world to wherever the teacher wants to lead them.

Again, this is not so much a substantive matter as a matter of being subtly appropriate. It is a matter of using the right examples, emphasizing the right aspects, shading the insights to meet certain needs, formulating the analogies that speak to their knowledge, experience, and penchants. And, needless to say, there is some relevance between this kind of awareness and doing biomedical ethics, namely: understanding the nuances of a situation is often crucial to giving an accurate moral analysis of that situation.

IV. Other Settings

Bioethics has wide relevance and wide interest. Thus far we have considered it from the rather narrow perspective of its teaching in medical school. We have done this for several reasons: medical schools have been the setting for the recent resurgence of interest in bioethics; it was believed that, given limited space, one setting should be examined in detail rather than exploring superficially many settings; and the medical is by far the most difficult setting for instituting bioethics teaching.

It was also believed that by seeing the details of introducing biomedical ethics to the variables and vicissitudes of medical schools, the reader would more easily be able to make the transitions to his or her own setting. Nevertheless, it is important to draw attention to the existence of different contexts and to the need and potential for adapting issues, methods, and emphases to various situations.

A. Nursing

As a small part of nursing's general declaration of professional independence from physicians, some have sought to lay claim even to unique ethical problems. Although the uniqueness might be a difficult claim to defend, there are somewhat different moral dilemmas to be faced. The issue usually cited as illustrating the difference concerns the nurse as subordinate in a system of patient care. Specifically, then, the dilemma is loyalty to the system or physician vs. moral obligation to the patient, patient's family, or society. This dilemma, of course, is not unique. A physician is often in an analogous situation vis-a-vis the system, and it is perhaps the most frequent moral dilemma in the business world.

The larger issues of bioethics are as relevant for nursing as for anyone else. This is true even for those issues wherein the nurse does not have ultimate responsibility for the decision. If the nurse it to help others think through the issues, to be a morally knowledgeable and sensitive member of the health-care team, and to be able to assess the loyalty vs. moral obligation conflict, then he or she can profit considerably from the study of biomedical ethics.

Pedagogically, it is almost always advantageous to approach the study of ethics by way of those problems which are or will be faced by the students. Thus, each group (dentists, nurses, nurse practitioners, physician assistants, patient-care specialists, radiologists, pharmacists, and so on) will develop its own key issues and cases, but seldom will these be different in principle from those faced by other groups.

Needless to say, there are also advantages to having these diverse groups in bioethics classes together, particularly if they are groups who will ordinarily encounter each other in their professional work. It stretches their moral imagination to have to see things from another's point of view; tolerance and respect for each other seem to be nurtured. However, there is a point of diminishing return on uniting the diverse groups. When the focuses and interests are too scattered, nothing jells—neither enthusiasm nor concepts nor purpose.

Nursing can use many of the formats discussed already—clinical experiences, grand rounds, bedside teaching. They should be raising the particular issues that concern them, even though in principle the cases may not be all that different.

B. Allied Health Programs

As in medicine and in nursing, allied health programs would take on their own character by building around the issues of particular concern to their practitioners. These programs currently seem rather fluid; new lines, distinctions, and roles are being drawn. Some are currently establishing criteria for licensure or certification, and are considering courses in ethics as a requirement. (The physician assistant program in New York State is a case in point where such decisions are pending.) Three significant strands are converging: search for professional identity, concern over professional responsibility, and a wave of interest in teaching ethics. While one can rejoice that these serious matters are receiving appropriate attention, one nevertheless worries that the convergence could produce too many requirements, proliferation of codification, teaching ethics as though it were a catechism, and general loss of that intellectual enrichment which ought to be part of genuine ethical inquiry.

In some of the allied health programs, a baccalaureate degree is not required. This sometimes means that the whole load of liberal arts will come in a single course or two. Ethics will then be placed somewhere in that potpourri. In light of that frequent eventuality, the plea is for a segment of cleanly done ethics, which is clear and distinct and not just part of a general celebration of human values. That is, even if it amounts to only two or three sessions, something helpful and provocative about moral concepts and ethical reasoning can be neatly demonstrated. Perhaps this could be done by following through on a single case, pushing it to some underlying principles and to the justification of those principles, and varying the parameters of the particular case enough to see the role of the morally relevant factors, thereby at least getting a hint of moral reasoning beyond the particular case. In short, when there is only a small amount of time, or when dilution by other humanistic studies (and often by social sciences) is threatened, ethics is better served by doing a small amount clearly and fully, rather than attempting to cover huge amounts with faint generalities.

C. Undergraduates

By far the most courses in bioethics are in the undergraduate curriculum. At least 1,000 colleges have at least one course in bioethics. Such a course can be found in philosophy or religion or biology departments; it is often team-taught.

There is an important sense in which the undergraduate bio-ethics course can be "purer." That is, it can be more of a liberal arts enterprise. Undergraduates seldom expect immediate clarity, relevance, and helpfulness as compared with the professional school student. Undergraduates are more apt to grant the teacher the time and their willing suspension of disbelief, enabling more elaborate, more sophisticated, more academically sound conceptual frameworks to be erected. They might tolerate a whole semester on abortion, whereas a professional school student would not. The student of a profession is far more pragmatic; he or she must reach a decision, there is not much time for intellectual play—no matter how valuable it would be in the long run. Ethics for the professional school student must compete with his other courses on grounds of helpfulness and practicality.

By the same token, the lack of urgency can be something of a stumbling block for undergraduates. They may have no experience of, or exposure to, the dramatic forcefulness of some of the bioethical issues. Exposure to clinical settings and to patients, discussion with the central figures in these dilemmas, and vicarious experience through novels, films, and case studies can add an important pedagogical edge.

The undergraduate can be led toward broader horizons; he can be led to see or try or do various problems without the immediate demand for relevance. Bioethics in that setting can be the occasion and vehicle of wider, more comprehensive intellectual endeavors, appropriate for undergraduate liberal arts education, though one would hope that the seriousness of ethics and the rigor of ethical reasoning would not be lost in the process.

The undergraduate is more open to whatever topics the professor finds conducive to attaining the goals of the course. An immediately pending profession is not dictating the student's interest. The undergraduate will also spend more time reading and writing for the course, since for her or him it is as valid and as relevant as any other course she or he is taking. So there is a sense in which an undergraduate might go more deeply into the course. On the other hand, absent is the passion for solving the problems which one frequently finds among professional school students, inasmuch as they know they will soon have to deal with that very problem "in real life."

D. Graduate

Bioethics reaches into many aspects of graduate education. It will suffice simply to mention these, since—with one exception—those engaged in graduate education in bioethics would already be beyond what we have to offer here. We will begin with the exception.

1. Residency

An excellent time for exposure to medical ethics is during the residency. It is an extremely influential time in the professional's development, and a time of enormous stress. The work load in caring for patients is very heavy, and the responsibility for clinical decisions is awesome. Additionally, the resident is totally absorbed in and frightened by the technology. He or she is terribly anxious about competence in techniques and procedures. Any plan for teaching ethics in such circumstances must work in, around, and with those givens. The "givens" are oppressively immense in the first year of residency and, generally, subside gradually with each successive year.

The format for teaching ethics in the residency setting would depend a great deal on the structure of the residency's formal teaching program. That is, if formal teaching sessions are already established, ethics might be integrated with those. But it would no doubt be most effective if the ethical issues were identified and thought about in the midst of caring for patients, and then pursued in more depth at a time set aside for that purpose. In other words, the ethics teacher should be right there in the action with the resident. The resident needs that support, and needs to know that the teacher really understands what the issues are. Under the intense pressure of gaining technological competence, classrooms and the more abstract issues are not apt to be meaningful to residents. More likely they would be seen as obstructive and counterproductive. Yet residents are keenly in need of the kind of counsel and perspective that biomedical ethics can provide. It seems imperative to meet them at least halfway.

Biomedical ethics in the context of residency training would very likely take on a wider scope, dealing as much with attitudes, emotions, styles, and other such matters that might more properly be described as a "philosophy of life" than as ethics. It is a ripe opportunity for wise, sensitive, seasoned teaching to make a crucial difference.

Under the auspices of the Society for Health and Human Values a major conference, The National Invitational Conference on Human Values Teaching in Primary Care Residency Training Programs, will be held in 1980 to examine ways to introduce human values education into residency training. Probably the first such conference of its kind, it will focus on primary-care residencies, that is, residencies in internal medicine, pediatrics, family medicine, and obstetrics-gynecology.

2. Nonmedical Professional Schools

Law, Divinity, Public Policy and Public Administration. These schools would raise bioethical issues as a way of shedding light on their own discipline as well as contributing the insights of their profession to the solution of bioethical problems. For example, it would be an occasion for law schools to reflect on the relationship of law to ethics in order to discover what law already says or implies (or can be made to say or imply) about these issues, and to see how much needs to be done (or not done) by law with respect to these issues.

Much the same integration of the biomedical issues with the issues and goals of the profession in question would take place in the other professional school contexts, in preparing one as counselor, policymaker, legislator, or whatever.

3. Graduate-level Study in Bioethics

Though there is an enormous demand for graduate work by those who want to teach in the field, fewer than a dozen places exist that offer this opportunity. There may be some question as to whether or not it is a field of sufficient depth to require graduate training. (See section VI-A, below.) One can always take further work in ethics within graduate philosophy or religion departments, but concentrating specifically on bioethics is seldom possible. (Unless such concentration means writing one's thesis or dissertation in that field, and until recently, even that probably would not have been acceptable in most philosophy departments.) These programs are still finding their way but ultimately will

probably include a good deal of straight ethics, a general understanding of the relevant sciences, and some clinical involvement.
At this juncture in the development of bioethics, it would probably be best to remain relatively fluid with respect to the ingre-
dients of such graduate study. The mixture of biology, medicine,
genetics, sociology, economics, philosophy of medicine, ethics,
and clinical exposure needs to be experimented with much more
before it should be allowed to jell. It may be best for each
candidate to fashion his or her own program, picking and choos-
ing according to previous training, needs, goals, and the various
strengths of the university where the work is to be done.

V. The State of the Art

Here we will report in a general way on what is happening around the country in the teaching of biomedical ethics. The field is growing so rapidly that there is no way to state the last word on its status: before the word can be uttered, the status has changed. This report is not the result of a survey undertaken just for this writing; it is actually a composite report gleaned from several sources surveyed within the last three or four years. Along with the extent of the teaching of biomedical ethics, we will also glimpse some of the settings in which it takes place and the topics customarily dealt with.

A. Medical Schools

The recent rebirth of medical ethics began about ten years ago (roughly around 1970) and its incubation was primarily in medical schools. According to a survey done by Robert Veatch and Sharmon Sollitto in 1974,[8] 97 of the 107 schools that responded indicated that some form of medical ethics teaching was taking place at their school. (There were at that time 112 medical schools in the country that were members of the American Association of Medical Colleges.) An earlier survey done in 1972 by Veatch revealed 81 schools engaged in some form of medical ethics teaching.[9] The growth in the two years between the surveys seems to indicate a significant surge in interest and commitment. The number of faculty devoting 50 percent or more of its

time to the teaching of medical ethics jumped from 19 to 31—
almost a 50 percent increase in those two years. Indicative of this
fast-rising interest was the tripling of special conferences and lectures devoted to those topics. This jumped from 17 in 1972 to 56
in 1974, and indicative of the continuing solid commitment was
the almost 30 percent increase in the number of formal courses
offered in medical ethics (37 in 1972; 47 in 1974).

By way of comparison and further documenting of this phenomenon, it should be noted that in 1976, 80 percent of the nursing schools (which both have an accredited baccalaureate
program and replied to the questionnaire) indicated they were
providing some planned opportunities for the study of nursing
ethics. This represents a third of the baccalaureate nursing programs in the country paying some attention to the study of ethics.[10]

Teaching ethics in medical schools is done in a large variety of
forms and formats. Sometimes it is said to "pervade" other
courses, sometimes it is a segment or module of other courses.
These other courses can be anything from "Introduction to Medicine" to " Human Behavior." Sometimes it is said to take place
only on "clerkships" in the interaction between teacher-clinician
and student-apprentice while involved in the actual care of patients. There are clerkships, usually a month in duration, devoted
entirely to the student's individual pursuit of the study of a particular issue within medical ethics. Some have a speakers' series
or a panel discussion series that is open to the entire medical
community.

However, courses dedicated to the specific topics of medical
ethics are the most frequent, and probably the most stable method
of teaching ethics in medical schools, as is advocated in the Report of The Hasting Center Project on the Teaching of Ethics.[11]
But the form and format of these are also diverse. They can be
elective or required, lecture or discussion, taught by "ethicists"
or clinicians. Furthermore, these courses can be found under the
auspices of a variety of departments: family medicine, psychiatry,
behavioral science, et al. It is difficult to generalize about medical schools. Their political and power structures, location, funding, and geographical and administrative relationship to other
schools and to a parent university make each one unique. Thus

innovative programs must be very individual, tailor-made for the school in question, as to department location, funding, and manpower. The courses utilize a variety of methods including lectures, discussions, self-study, films, simulated games, and journal article reviews.

A growing phenomenon in medical education is the "Department of Humanities," or the "Human Values in Medicine Program." There are probably about 40 of them now in existence in approximately 115 medical schools.[12] (And one has the impression that there are probably as many more in various stages of planning and development.) These endeavors are much broader than the study of medical ethics alone; they are attempts to do with and for many human values what has been described earlier for ethical values. But more accurately, these are attempts of the various humanistic disciplines individually to use their particular skills, data, and methods to enhance the understanding and effectiveness of medicine in all its aspects. And similarly, these disciplines find themselves enriched through their efforts to interact with medicine.

These programs often cross other disciplinary lines. Some function for the entire health-education complex, which can include nursing, allied health professions, dentistry, pharmacy, and even veterinary medicine. Medical ethics is almost always one of the basics offered to each group. And for each group the actual moral dilemmas confronted are, of course, somewhat different. Nevertheless, they probably still have more in common than they have differences, but it is more meaningful to each group to approach ethics through the specific problems of its own expertise and experience. Indeed, one can even detect at times a matter of pride that one's own field has its unique moral problems, not to be identified or assimilated to those of another group. (E.g., this has been expressed on occasion by those representing nursing.)

The field of biomedical ethics, however, even goes outside the health professions. At some universities such a course has been the occasion for uniting schools of law, divinity, and medicine in a single endeavor. The content of biomedical ethics holds interest for nearly everyone, and profits from perspectives and insights from a variety of fields. In fact, it is true that most teaching of bioethics takes place outside professional health education.

Schools of law, divinity, public policy, and public administration account for many of these, but by far the largest number are in the undergraduate schools, and there they can be found in a variety of departments: religion, philosophy, biology, natural sciences, and social sciences.

B. Undergraduate Schools

Two surveys of a sort have been done, and although they do not really agree with each other, noting some of their findings can give us a picture of what is going on (as well as the difficulty in surveying it). One survey limited itself to schools offering at least a baccalaureate degree and enrolling at least 5,000 students. Among United States colleges and universities 360 met these criteria and were sent questionnaires; 62 percent or 223 completed and returned the questionnaires. The results were published in 1977 by Jon Hendrix.[13] The second survey, unpublished, was done by Carola Mone for The Hastings Center. In this survey a large sample of 1977 and 1978 college catalogs were examined to find course titles or descriptions that would indicate that ethics or values was a major or minor theme in that course. The survey included 623 course catalogs, that is, approximately 27 percent of all senior educational institutions in the United States (623 out of 2,270).

Inasmuch as these surveys are of different types, there is not much concurrence between them. Hendrix used questionnaires, and sent them only to schools with 5,000 or more students; and it was done about a year earlier than Mone's; Mone sampled catalogs, which are often slow to reflect recent changes. Hendrix found a total of 58 courses in bioethics being given; Mone found that almost *all* of her sampling of 623 schools offered a course in "bioethics" or "ethics and the life sciences"! By even conservative extrapolation from Mone's study we could estimate well over 1,500 colleges offering courses in bioethics. That would also be a low estimate because college catalogs are quite late in reflecting changes. (Mone points out that coincidentally she discovered one school was in actuality offering 35 more courses in ethics than were listed in its course catalogue!) To give perspective on the rise of bioethics, Mone points out that an informal survey of catalogs from 1950-65 revealed practically no such courses in existence.

Hendrix reports that 45 percent of the bioethics courses are taught within biology departments. Though Mone does not speak to that particular point, nothing she observes would be inconsistent with it. She does note that in her sampling, 25 percent of all the ethics courses taught (this included Theoretical Ethics, as well as Ethics of Business, of Law, of Journalism, and so on) were taught within philosophy departments.

This brief unsatisfying excursion into surveys is only to give a gross indicator of the extent and speed with which courses in biomedical ethics are developing. In fact it is so extensive and so rapid that accurate surveys do not seem to be possible.

C. Some Usual and Unusual Topics

By perusing the many course syllabi sent into The Hastings Center and by studying the publication of the American Association for the Advancement of Science titled *EVIST Resource Directory* (a directory of programs and courses in Ethics and Values in Science and Technology) one can get a good sense of what topics are being treated, and how.[14]

Inasmuch as ethics and values considerations cut through all disciplines, one finds a wide variety of learning "arrangements." Sometimes "biomedical ethics" represents only a small portion of a study of applied ethics or of value studies in general; sometimes it is the main focus. Some use biomedical ethics as an introit into heavier philosophical topics; others use it for its own understanding; still others use it as a springboard to do more biology or genetics, elaborating the relevant details of those sciences more than the ethical theory. Actually, biomedical concerns can relate to nearly everything—environment, population, politics, religion. And consequently they are made to do so. One suspects that because biomedical matters have a cutting edge and because they intimately concern us, they make enticing avenues into wider, broader, and more remote matters.

We must distinguish between programs and courses. In the

health professional schools one can often find bioethics and/or human values programs that have many emphases and methods and courses. This is a total approach to understanding and assimilating human values and is generally meant to have an influence on and perhaps to provide a service for the health-medical complex of which it is a part. For a more comprehensive description of these, the reader is referred to the document, *Human Values Teaching Programs for Health Professionals* (see Bibliography).

The goals for offering courses are almost universally the same, although professional schools may make them a bit more explicit by reference to performance as professionals. The goals always cite the need to raise the consciousness of students, that is, to increase their awareness of the moral problems, and beyond that to help the students become more knowledgeable, adept, and articulate in the processes of moral reasoning.

The typical topics dealt with are as follows: behavioral control (behavior modification, drugs, psychosurgery, psychiatry), confidentiality, truth-telling, informed consent, distribution of scarce resources, termination of life (euthanasia), decisions concerning defective newborns, right to have and to refuse treatment, experimentation on humans (especially children, prisoners, the unconscious, the institutionalized), genetic counseling, genetic engineering (cloning, recombinant DNA), organ donations and transplants, definitions of death, and public policy considerations of all of the foregoing issues. These issues appear in a variety of combinations and orderings; sometimes the entire course is devoted to only one of the topics. But far more frequently four-fifths of those topics would appear in any one biomedical ethics course.

Some of the less typical items dealt with in such courses are these: advertising of drugs, suicide, population control, conflict between individual and society, the medical-social issues (and the involvement of medical definitions, economic theory, and societal beliefs), iatrogenicity, rights of patients, effects of biomedical technology (on patients, on delivery of care, on taxpayers, and on society in general), relationship of minorities to the health-care system, political psychiatry, biohazards, sperm banking and artificial insemination, surrogate motherhood, comparison of the "answers" given by different religious traditions (to the biomedical ethical issues), strikes and the health professions, rights of the public with respect to scientific research, research strategies (ethics of research design, value conflicts between subject, researcher, and society). Different specialty schools will very likely include topics particularly relevant to their own profession; for example, a medical school might include: professional codes, styles of medical practice, aims of medical practice, physician competence, implications of "profession" for the doctor/patient relationship, who owns the patient's medical record, dealing with chronically ill patients and their families, dealing with dying, death, and grief, the physician as sexuality counselor.

As a rule these more unusual topics are included when there is no course specifically dealing with biomedical ethics. In professional schools one frequently finds one general course attempting to include all the "nonhard-core material. There is a smattering of social, psychological, legal, ethical aspects of medicine and health care. In the context of those courses "ethics" is not so sharply or technically defined; the focus is more on general awareness of all these other factors and not so particularly on ethics and moral reasoning.

VI. Some Problematic Issues

A. How "Deep" Is Biomedical Ethics?

On the surface it is not clear either why or how one should take depth soundings. It has not been talked about head-on, yet a scattering of implications, insinuations, and inferences surround this issue. It is difficult even to describe what the issue is. It is adumbrated by such questions as these: Can anyone teach ethics? Are there "experts" in ethics? Doesn't the intellectual challenge of professional ethics in a professional school pale significantly by comparison to the professional courses? Is "applied ethics" even a respectable field?

This writer has long held the belief that one has only to scratch the surface of biomedical ethics and he is immediately in the realm of "straight" ethics. Thus, if there is ethical "depth" to biomedical ethics it is the same as the "depth" one finds in ethics in general. This would include ethical theories, metaethics, foundations of ethics, and the epistemological concerns of ethics.

This same point can be made in a more understandable way. Consider if it would be reasonable to develop a Ph.D. program in medical ethics. What would the program be like? It would seem that it would be broad rather than deep. That is, one might be exposed to biology, genetics, medicine, health-care delivery systems, health-economic and social theory, and so on, but the *ethics* utilized on each issue would not necessarily be "advanced" or "deep." The facts and theories of the various fields whose morality is being investigated may indeed be vast and difficult, but the ethical expertise and theory for dealing with them need not be. And insofar as the ethics aspects are conceptually pressed further, one enters the arena of "regular" philosophical ethics. This would seem to be a corollary to the claim that biomedical ethics is not a special kind of ethics, but simply ethics being applied to a special area of concerns.[15] The area of concerns is individuated by whatever sets off "biomedical" from other domains, and, in any case, it is so set off by principles or characteristics *other than* the moral concerns and ethical principles found there.

This is not to say that biomedical ethics—or any field of "applied ethics"—is therefore shallow and superficial. It is instead to suggest that the specifically moral reasoning that goes on there may not be deep and difficult. The difficulty is rather in the meticulous understanding of the field to which the ethics is being applied. The concepts, behavior, beliefs, strategies, and goals of that field must be understood, analyzed, clarified, and probed in order for the ethical reasoning to be "applied" with relevance and accuracy. This kind of "ground preparation" for doing ethics might itself be considered ethics. It is certainly part of the enterprise of *applied* ethics, but it need not presuppose a very sophisticated level of ethical theory or foundations. For example, that we ought not kill is a straightforward moral rule. But whether or not withholding or withdrawing resuscitative efforts is an instance of killing involves one in facts, nuance, distinctions, and analysis. Similarly, a careful, astute explication of the meaning of paternalism may be called for before anything very helpful can be said about its morality, and very likely the moral theory employed to remark on its morality need not be nearly as sophisticated as the explication of the concept. Such analysis, definitions, distinctions, and juxtapositions might require considerable insight, knowledge, and general philosophical acumen, but that does not make the enterprise ethics *per se.* (Although undoubtedly ethical theory subtly influences the "ground preparation"; so the two endeavors are not unrelated.)

Basically what is being suggested in this section is twofold: that the field of biomedical ethics (and probably any other field of applied ethics) is much broader than it is deep in terms of philosophical ethics (ethical theory, ethical foundations, metaethics) and that the difficult and sophisticated work, if it is done at all, is in analyzing the circumstances that are to be morally appraised. Though on the surface this suggestion may seem trivial, it is interesting when related to a variety of observations and considerations.

(1) Consider the philosophical or theological "purists" who dismiss the entire enterprise of applied ethics as not being "real ethics" and as not being intellectually and academically respectable. With respect to traditional ethics—the foundations, epistemology, and metaethics—they may well be right, but what they miss is the rigor and careful analysis that goes into "ground preparation." This is something the "purist" never had to do, inasmuch as he spent all his time on sharpening theoretical tools and no time on using them in real situations. In focusing on "real situations," we are discovering a complexity and need for explication and analysis never imagined by the theoretician—because he never looked.

(2) The literature of biomedical ethics can be frustrating, particularly to philosophers, in that dozens of articles on the "same" topic may all utilize an ordinary unsophisticated level of moral theory. At worst, they differ, if at all, only in this or that additional fact or emphasis; at best they differ by virtue of a different conceptual analysis of the situation in question. There comes to be a kind of one-upsmanship with respect to the facts and nuances of the circumstances being morally examined, but this is of little interest to the ethical theorist who finds therein nothing conceptually intriguing or challenging. The truth of the matter is that many of these articles *are* alike. This is very likely because part of the mission of applied ethics is to raise the consciousness of many different groups. So, like a sermon, the same basic content is apt to be repeated over and over in the same and different places. Awareness, not new and different conceptual analyses, is the point.

For example, consider the issue of informed consent. Endless articles say essentially the same thing; seldom is anything conceptually new accomplished—that is, in terms of moral theory; but the need for informed consent is uncovered and emphasized in new circumstances and settings. At their intellectual and conceptual best, biomedical ethics articles will interestingly explore or extend or challenge ethical theories in light of the details of biomedicine, or they will provide new and perceptive analyses of those details, so that the implications of the old and familiar morality (whatever that might be) can be more accurately "applied," or more decisively rejected.

(3) This issue of "depth" may also account for the differences of opinion with respect to the credentials and training of teachers. If the moral theory aspects are not deep, then great familiarity with the facts, concepts, and behavior of the enterprise in question is what is most necessary. If one goes deeply into moral theory, it seems incommensurate with the practical issues being decided within the particular enterprise. It is analysis beyond necessity. There appears a gap between the subtleties and sophistication of high level ethics and the practical moral conflicts to be resolved within a field. The fine points of the former seem to have no relevance for decisions in the latter. Consequently, knowledge of the field is stressed more than sophistication in ethics. To some in professional education, the ethics of their field is seen as an embarrassment, precisely because it seems to be at a much lower conceptual level from the level of study in the profession itself—law, economics, business, social policy, and so on. Ethics can of course be done at a very high level, but then it loses its close connection and integration with the profession's practical moral problems which are in need of solution. This will be more true of some fields than others. Some, such as political theory and public policy, could helpfully and without disparity spend considerable time on the theoretical level of ethics, as this is on a level and of a kind with the substance of the field itself. Medicine, on the other hand, would be a field where extensively developing the fine details of ethical theory would be much less appropriate.

What is being overlooked in this either/or situation is training for the skill of "ground preparation." Just knowing a field or enterprise very well is not in itself enough. A physician may know a great deal about dying and the criteria of death, about medically screening patients for dialysis, about laboratory test results, and still not be aware of or articulate about the value and moral issues involved. Such naiveté may also be true of one schooled in ethical theory. "Ground preparation" requires the ability to define, explicate, classify, and distinguish elements and aspects of a field so as to uncover the moral questions and the morally relevant factors. Some knowledge of the field is necessary but not sufficient. Some knowledge of ethical theory and metaethics is necessary but not sufficient. What it is that is necessary and sufficient is hard to describe, but one very general answer might be: experience and sophistication in applied ethics. Perhaps it is the "ground preparation" which is the essence of applied ethics, and to be done well, it requires more analytical skills and rigor than is generally thought.

B. Indoctrination

Indoctrination is an accusation that often follows on the heels of any proposal to teach ethics, and it is one that is considered not only here but in the Report of The Hastings Center Project on the Teaching of Ethics.[16] This seems particularly pervasive in professional schools, and most particularly, it is a worry of faculty members other than ethics teachers. Though one could explicate this concern and turn it into a series of precise claims to be replied to, it seems more appropriate to our goals here simply to take this worry over indoctrination at its ordinary, imprecise, but spirited face value, and attempt to allay those misgivings.

The overarching worry is that the students will be led to a particular position on each of the controversial issues of the field—namely, that position espoused by the instructor. Included in this worry is that indoctrination into a general leaning or suasion will take place—leftist, conservative, pro-life, liberal, and so on.

Scratch the surface of that general worry and one will usually find some vague, loosely held beliefs about the nature of morality. One is that morality is largely subjective, that each person has his own "ethical beliefs," and that probably one is as good as any other (since objective validation is impossible). The other vague belief is that in ethics classes, students are particularly susceptible to indoctrination, putty in the hands of an opinionated ethics teacher.

Although the preceding are positions this writer would want to rephrase precisely and then refute, that is not necessary for present purposes. Instead, one who shares these worries should be reassured about what goes on in a good ethics course. As in any course, everything must be subjected to the light of reason. Everything can be questioned, and attempted answers must be defended. The very worries we are now addressing (roughly, "Is ethics completely subjective?") would be raised for discussion, and arguments for and against would be developed and worked through. The goal is to train students to question and pursue moral issues with as much rigor as the field admits, and to be able to assess the strengths and weaknesses of moral reasoning. It is precisely these emphases that would keep the students from becoming foils for an indoctrinator. The reasoning skills and knowledge gained in class are those that direct the student toward independence in thinking, and could just as easily be used to disagree with the teacher. The reader should review the "Paraphrased Class Discussion" (II-C above) to regain a sense of how an ethics class unfolds, and to see whether and where indoctrination could take place. It is evident that students are pressed to understand their own positions (the foundations and validations for these positions); to understand the position of others in the classroom (and how those positions are defended); and to be able to articulate precisely where the nub of disagreement is between themselves and anyone else with whom they are disagreeing.

There are those who would argue that methodological indoctrination nevertheless takes place. That is, inasmuch as students are taught to analyze, look for reasons, construct arguments, criticize and defend, just so far are they being prejudiced in favor of what might be called a liberal, intellectual world view. This is, for example, opposed to accepting things on faith, on tradition, or on authority.

However, even that is not clearly true. In studying ethics one is looking at lines of reasoning, and some lines might be at bottom matters of faith, tradition, or authority. Discovering precisely where, if at all, these enter into one's reasoning processes, is part of what the study of ethics is concerned with.

The antagonist could still insist, nevertheless, that by the course's stress on reasoning rather than on the unquestioning acceptance of pronouncements by faith, tradition, or authority, it is indoctrinating in a point of view. The best answer to this may be an appeal to semantics. Leading people to think and reason for themselves is what *education* is. Instilling conclusions and positions that are not open to reasoning and questioning is what *indoctrination* is, and it is not appropriate in an educational setting. It may be "training," "instilling," "conditioning," "catechizing"—but it is not *education*.

C. Reformer or Teacher?

There are those who urge that teachers of ethics must at the same time be reformers. They must give embodiment to their abstractions; be living testimony to their theories. It is argued that a "moral presence" is what is needed, a prophet in their midst, a force for the good, a stellar example. An ethics teacher who does not take stands, who does not speak out, who runs no risks is one who will not be taken seriously, nor will the field be properly represented. This writer is not one who would so argue, at least not if by "reformer" we mean one who exposes and declaims people and practices, and openly leads the forces for change.

What would be lost in confusing the roles of teacher and reformer would be the true teacher role—the objective eye, the moderator, the calm resource of reason. What is needed in the complicated and emotion-laden issues of biomedical ethics is rigorous and systematic guidance. There must be an arena in which matters can be openly, thoroughly, and honestly discussed. To become a reformer would be to politicize the classroom, indeed, the entire medical center. Credibility and trust would be lost.

Issues that are proper fodder for a reformer are issues that are clearly immoral; they are generally conceptually uncomplicated. The immorality is clear and distinct, and change is called for. The teacher's role, on the other hand, is to help work through complicated matters—sorting out, analyzing, clarifying, and explicating concepts, principles, lines of reasoning, commitments, and foundations.

This is not to say that the ethics teacher ought not to take stands. He or she should be no less a conscientious citizen, faculty member, human being, committee worker than anyone else. But this role should be kept separate from the teaching role. One who mounts a platform at the drop of a hat will not be one to whom others turn for guidance and instruction. That person is more apt to become a tool than a teacher.

One suspects that *motivation* to be moral happens more by example than by teaching ethics. It is not clear that it is the job of an ethics teacher to motivate students to be moral. Would he or she have failed as a teacher if the students were not so motivated? The teacher can model *seriousness* toward moral matters, and thus motivate students to take these matters seriously, to realize that there is something important at stake. That is not the same as making them be moral or motivating them to be moral. But being a good example for something is appropriate and possible in the teaching situation, and in the long run, modeling a serious, thoughtful approach to moral issues may very well be more valuable than setting an example as Resident Reformer.

Professional and undergraduate schools may have an interesting difference on this score. It somehow seems more fitting in a professional school that the teacher actually stand for or ex-emplify certain values, when appropriate. Thus, the ethics teacher who is also clinician should (with patients or as department head or administrative officer) manifest moral behavior, as indeed would be desired of all clinicians, whether they are ethics teachers or not. The profession itself is committed to certain values and behavior known in advance by those entering the profession. The professional school may very well see as part of its obligation to the public the inculcation of these values in the students-to-be-practitioners. In that sense the professional school is not the totally open, "value-free" institution of learning that other kinds of schools might claim to be.

Contrariwise, an undergraduate school, or a graduate school in liberal arts (depending on its stated goals), might not find it untoward at all to have someone teaching ethics who in fact believes the whole field is silly, wrong, or impossible, or who is himself immoral. As long as the theories and foundations and reasoning of ethics were being presented, the teaching alone would be sufficient. Of course, the school may have *other* values it might insist on being exemplified, such as serious scholarship or intellectual integrity.

We started this section by wondering if the teacher must be a reformer. The answer, at least for those teaching in medical or allied health-professional schools, is that it is neither necessary nor advisable, lest effectiveness as teacher be lost. But this is not to say that he or she should not take stands on issues that are appropriate to other roles in which they serve, nor is it to underplay the importance of example for motivating moral behavior. But it is to question the appropriateness and wisdom of teacher *as teacher* to be motivator of moral behavior in ways that risk effectiveness as teacher.

D. Religious vs. Philosophical Ethics

The identification and interrelationship of these disciplines goes back thousands of years. The reader will be spared even the most cursory glimpse of that rich and complicated past. Our present concern is instead practical: thumbnail sketches that might help the administrator see the various strengths and slants of both approaches, inasmuch as the two might be contending for the teaching of biomedical ethics.

Religious ethics, as discussed earlier, would (or should) be an attempt to look at moral problems from a religious perspective. That is, one attempts to resolve a moral issue according to one or another religion's precepts. The moral implications of these precepts are often difficult to see, so that establishing and interpreting the religious precepts can become a major matter of attention.

A philosopher, on the other hand, would try to construct the theoretical framework of morals on beliefs that all rational people could accept. Morality to them would necessarily be something that all persons should participate in, not just those who are led to accept this or that metaphysical belief.

Each approach has its advantages. The philosopher need not presume any kind of religious commitment or interest on the student's part. His or her doing of ethics is independent of religion. On the other hand, many students (and patients) already have religious beliefs and are anxious to see what their faith has to say about particular moral problems. Such motivation and interest at the start provide a good foundation on which a teacher can build.

But the teacher's job should be able to be taken on by either a philosopher or theologian, trained in ethical theory. Either should be able to start at the point the student has reached in his thinking and train him in ferreting out the issues, explicating the necessary concepts, developing and following out lines of reasoning, formulating and working with basic principles. Much of this can be done independently of any religious beliefs. The teacher's role, in any case, is not to indoctrinate, but to help the student understand the taxonomy of moral reasoning, how and where things fit in, including items of faith.

In short, religion and philosophy in doing ethics would develop many similar categories, maneuvers, and analyses. One could be significantly helped in understanding ethics by either approach. Ethics does not need a religious foundation, but some find it important. Reasoning through the ins and outs of such claims can be interesting and clarifying, as can be the differences of action that might result if one accepted one or the other foundation. One suspects that serious ethical theories would probably not be in conflict over what a moral agent should do in most situations, but would disagree only over the explanation of *why* they should so act.

Appendix

Resources (A Starter Kit)

This section is meant to be a kind of introductory package for those in the early stages of teaching bioethics. It makes no attempt to be complete. Each source mentioned will lead to numerous additional sources, making a spider web of references and connections.

A. References and Bibliographical Sources

1. *Encyclopedia of Bioethics,* ed. Warren T. Reich (New York: The Free Press, 1978). This is a four-volume work, international in scope, covering the major concepts and aspects of bioethics. Each of the 300 articles has a bibliography. It is well organized for easy and accurate use.
2. *Dictionary of Medical Ethics,* A. S. Duncan, G. R. Dunstan, and R. B. Welbourn (London: Darton, Longman and Todd, 1977). This is a little more than a dictionary, though a good bit less than an encyclopedia. A quick and easy reference for summary descriptions.
3. *Annotated Bibliography of Bioethics,* ed. Madeline M. Nevins (Rockville, Md.: Information Planning Associates, Inc., 1977). This was related to a publishing project, *Bioethics Digest,* which was a very helpful journal, giving elaborate annotations of current articles. It was published from 1976–78.

4. *Bibliography of Bioethics,* ed. LeRoy Walters (Detroit: Gale Research Co.) This is an annual volume (beginning with 1973) which catalogs all the articles published each year in the field of bioethics. It has developed its own system of classification; it is helpful, clear, and easy to use.

5. *BIOETHICSLINE* is a computerized literature retrieval service of The National Library of Medicine. By using key words this system will print out the bibliographical information on all the current articles related to those key words. Its data base is cross-disciplinary, goes back to 1973, and is updated every four months. The data base is published annually as the *Bibliography of Bioethics.* Information on the BIOETHICSLINE Services can be obtained from most medical school libraries or from The Center for Bioethics at the Kennedy Institute for Ethics.

6. *Index Medicus.* This is published monthly by The National Library of Medicine. It is to the medical world what *Reader's Guide to Periodical Literature* is to the general reading public. Its key terms and classifications for ethics are of course not nearly so fine and precise as *Bibliography of Bioethics,* but grosser categories can be researched ("ethics," "euthanasia," "abortion," etc.). It has a very comprehensive data base, and it goes back many years.

7. There are of course all the other normal bibliographical tools that most readers are familiar with:
   Bibliographic Index
   The Philosopher's Index
   Humanities Index
   Index to Legal Periodicals

8. *The Hastings Center Bibliography* (Institute of Society, Ethics and the Life Sciences, 360 Broadway, Hastings-on-Hudson, N.Y. 10706). This is a very helpful compilation of selected articles and books, some of them annotated. It is well organized by topics; it also has an author index. It is updated from time to time. The most recent (as of this printing) is 1979–80.

9. Gorovitz, Samuel. *Medical Ethics Film Review Project* (College Park: University of Maryland, The Council for Philosophical Studies, 1974). This annotates some selected films available prior to 1974.

10. Trautmann, Joanne and Pollard, Carol. *Literature and Medicine: Topics, Titles and Notes* (Philadelphia: The Society for Health and Human Values, 925 Chestnut St. 19107, 1975). This is an annotated bibliography of literary works related to thirty-nine medical topics. It covers literature from the classical period to the twentieth century. It is a wealth of resources, and it is very well done.

B. Journals Largely Specializing in Bioethics

1. *The Hastings Center Report* (360 Broadway, Hastings-on-Hudson, N.Y. 10706). Undoubtedly, this publication has done more than any other to stimulate reflection on bioethical concerns. Earlier given primarily to short pieces, it has recently published longer and deeper articles.
2. *Ethics in Science and Medicine* (Pergamon Press, Maxwell House, Fairview Park, Elmsford, N.Y. 10523).
3. *Man and Medicine: The Journal of Values and Ethics in Health Care* (630 West 168th St., New York, New York, 10032).
4. *Journal of Medical Ethics* (Society for the Study of Medical Ethics, Tavistock House East, Tavistock Square, London WC1H 9LG, England).
5. *Linacre Quarterly* (National Federation of Catholic Physicians' Guilds, Dr. John P. Mullooly, 8430 W. Capitol Drive, Milwaukee, Wisc. 53222).
6. *Bioethics Quarterly* (Northwest Institute of Ethics and the Life Sciences, 6241 31st Ave., N.E., Seattle, Wash. 98115).
7. *Journal of Medicine and Philosophy* (Society for Health and Human Values, 925 Chestnut St., Philadelphia, Pa. 19107). This journal is generally devoted to the philosophy of medicine, but on occasion the theme of an issue is a medical ethics topic.

C. Other Professional Journals

These journals occasionally have articles dealing with bioethical concerns. They generally speak to the interests of the audience for the journal; that is, the articles in medical journals are written to be understandable and of interest to the medical community, the philosophy journals' articles have the interest of the philosophical audience as primary. For a particular emphasis, they are well worth regular perusal.

American Journal of Law and Medicine
American Journal of Medicine
American Journal of Nursing
American Journal of Public Health
American Journal of Psychiatry
Annals of Internal Medicine
Bioscience
British Medical Journal
Bulletin of the History of Medicine
Ethics
Journal of the American Medical Association (JAMA)
Journal of Medical Education
Journal of Religious Ethics
Lancet
Legal Medical Quarterly
Medical Care
Medical World News (A sort of *Time* magazine for medicine)
Milbank Memorial Fund Quarterly
New England Journal of Medicine
New Physician
Nursing
Nursing Forum
Nursing Outlook
Nursing Research
Perspectives in Biology and Medicine
Philosophy and Public Affairs
Public Interest
Science

Law School Reviews are excellent sources for occasional articles. However, no one of these journals has significantly more bioethics-related articles than any other.

Organizations

1. *Ethics Resource Center* (1730 Rhode Island Ave. NW, Suite

717, Washington, D.C. 20036.) As of this writing, this organization is in its infancy. It is attending primarily to the development of resources for professional ethics other than biomedical, such as journalism, business, engineering, law, because the biomedical is already well underway elsewhere.

2. *Committee for Philosophy and Medicine* (American Philosophical Association: Headquarters at University of Delaware, Newark, Delaware 19711). Formed as a committee of The American Philosophical Association to stimulate and to be a resource center for this new, emerging interest of some philosophers. It also publishes a newsletter, to which non-APA members may subscribe.

3. *The Hastings Center, Institute of Society, Ethics and the Life Sciences* (360 Broadway, Hastings-on-Hudson, N.Y. 10706). Founded in 1969 out of a growing concern over bioethical matters (especially, at that time, concern with issues surrounding genetic engineering, behavioral control, and death and dying), The Hastings Center obviously spoke to a deeply felt need, cross-disciplinary and international in scope. The Institute has prospered in staff and stature, as it has begun to fill the need for investigation of the biomedical revolution with all its ethical, legal, and social implications and quandaries. It has stimulated and advanced research and teaching in these areas of concern, and identified and developed intellectual, knowledgeable, and bibliographical resources for doing the task. Associate memberships, entitling one to many publications, including the *Hastings Center Report,* are available.

4. *The Joseph and Rose Kennedy Institute of Ethics* (Georgetown University, Washington, D.C. 20057). The Institute as a whole focuses on the technical, demographic, and ethical aspects of human reproduction. Within the Institute is *The Center for Bioethics,* which has a research staff in bioethics. They participate in a variety of research and teaching activities including Georgetown's postgraduate program in bioethics. The Center has an excellent library, and has developed a bioethics information retrieval system providing indexing, bibliographies, classification, and automated information retrieval (BIOETHICSLINE). Also within this context the *Encyclopedia of Bioethics* (4 vols. The Free press, 1978) was produced.

5. *Ministers in Medical Education* (Sixth Floor, 925 Chestnut

St., Philadelphia, Pa. 19107). This is an association, made up primarily of clergymen, interested in the issues of ministry in medical education. They began meeting in the late 1950s and have continued with annual meetings and programs for the sharing and stimulating of ideas. A newsletter is published. Membership is available to those who share these concerns.

6. *Northwest Institute of Ethics and the Life Sciences* (6241 31st Ave., N.E., Seattle, Wash. 98115). The Institute is an educational organization devoted to the study of bioethical and ethical issues. Its members include physicians, medical educators, health-care policymakers, theologians, and philosophers. The Institute offers courses and publishes *Bioethics Quarterly*.

7. *The Society for Health and Human Values* (Sixth Floor, 925 Chestnut St., Philadelphia, Pa. 19107). One of the pioneer groups of this field, the society began informally in 1963 as a gathering of medical educators sharing concerns and ideas about the role of human values in medical education. They met during the annual week's meetings of the Association of American Medical Colleges. The Society's interest is much broader than medical ethics, but it includes medical ethics. It has stimulated and provided considerable information, research, and publication on matters of health and human values; it has been instrumental in developing human-values teaching programs in health and medical professional schools. Memberships, entitling one to many publications, are available.

8. *Society for the Study of Medical Ethics* (Tavistock House East, Tavistock Square, London WC1H 9LG, England). Among other activities for stimulating and assisting with the study of medical ethics, the society publishes the *Journal of Medical Ethics*.

9. *Excellent sources of information are those schools with substantial programs in teaching bioethics in one form or another. Consult the EVIST Directory, Human Values Teaching Programs for Health Professionals* (Society for Health and Human Values), and *Ministers in Medical Education* (The Society for Health and Human Values). Among the oldest, largest, and most experienced, are the programs at Pennsylvania State University College of Medicine at Hershey, the

University of Texas Medical Branch at Galveston, The University of Tennessee Center for the Health Sciences at Memphis, Southern Illinois University School of Medicine at Springfield, Michigan State University College of Human Medicine at East Lansing, and University of Florida Medical School at Gainesville. There are also many undergraduate colleges that have developed programs of values or ethics, offering courses and/or generally pervading the curriculum. The EVIST Directory is a good source for locating such programs.

Notes

1. For a much fuller and suggestive discussion of the history of medical ethics education, see: Pellegrino, Edmund, "Medical Education"; Robert Veatch, "Medical Ethics Education"; and "Medical Ethics, History of," in *Encyclopedia of Bioethics,* ed. Warren T. Reich, (New York: The Free Press, 1978).

2. Reiser, Stanley J., "Humanism and Fact-Finding in Medicine," *New England Journal of Medicine* 299 (October 26, 1978), 950–53.

3. Jones, Marshall B., "Health Status Indexes: The Trade-Off Between Quantity and Quality of Life," *Socio-Economic Planning Sciences* 11, Pergamon Press, 1977, 301–305.

4. *The Teaching of Ethics in Higher Education: A Report by The Hastings Center* (Hastings-on-Hudson, N.Y.: The Hastings Center, 1980), pp. 47–52.

5. Clouser, K. Danner, "Medicine, Humanities, and Integrating Perspectives," *Journal of Medical Education* 52 (November 1977), 930–32.

6. *The Teaching of Ethics...,* pp. 54–55.

7. Ibid., pp. 62–66, 81–82.

8. Veatch, Robert, and Sollitto, Sharmon, "Medical Ethics Teaching: A Report of a National Medical School Survey," *Journal of the American Medical Association* 235 (March 8, 1976), 1030–33.

9. Veatch, Robert, "National Survey of the Teaching of Medical Ethics in Medical Schools," *The Teaching of Medical Ethics,* eds. R. Veatch, W. Gaylin, and C. Morgan (Hastings-on-Hudson, N.Y.: The Hastings Center, 1973), pp. 97–102.

10. Aroskar, Mila, "Ethics in the Nursing Curriculum," *Nursing Outlook* 25 (April 1977), 260–64. See also, Aroskar, Mila and Veatch, Robert, "Ethics Teaching in Nursing Schools," *The Hastings Center Report* 7 (August 1977), pp. 23–26.

11. *The Teaching of Ethics...,* p. 82.

12. See McElhinney, Thomas K., ed., *Human Values Teaching Programs for Health Professionals* (Philadelphia: The Society for Health and Human Values, 1976).

13. Hendrix, Jon R., "A Survey of Bioethics Courses in U.S. Colleges and Universities," *The American Biology Teacher* 39 (February 1977), 85ff.

14. *EVIST Resource Directory*, (Washington: American Association for the Advancement of Science, 1978).

15. Clouser, K. Danner, "What Is Medical Ethics," *Annuals of Internal Medicine* 80 (May 1974), 657–60. Also, Clouser, K. Danner, "Bioethics," *Encyclopedia of Bioethics,* ed. Warren T. Reich (New York: The Free Press, 1978), vol. 1, pp. 115–27.

16. *The Teaching of Ethics...,* pp. 55–62; 81.

Bibliography

1. On Teaching Bioethics

Aroskar, Mila A. "Ethics in The Nursing Curriculum," *Nursing Outlook* 25 (April 1977): 260–64.

———, and Veatch, Robert. "Ethics Teaching in Nursing Schools," *Hastings Center Report* 7 (August 1977): 23–26.

Bluestone, Naomi R. "Teaching of Ethics in Schools of Public Health," *American Journal of Public Health* 66 (May 1976): 478–79.

Brody, Howard. "Integrating Ethics into the Medical Curriculum: One School's Progress Report," *Michigan Medicine* (February 1975): 111–17.

———. "Teaching Medical Ethics: Future Challenges," *Journal of the American Medical Association* 229 (July 8, 1974): 177–79.

Clouser, K. Danner. "Humanities and the Medical School: A Sketched Rationale and Description," *British Journal of Medical Education* 5 (September 1971): 226–31.

———. *Philosophy and Medicine: Clinical Management of a Mixed Marriage.* Philadelphia: Society for Health and Human Values, 1972.

———. "Medicine, Humanities, and Integrating Perspectives," *Journal of Medical Education* 51 (November 1977): 930–32.

———. "Philosophy and Medical Education," *The Role of the Humanities in Medical Education.* Edited by Donnie J. Self. Norfolk, Virginia: Teagle and Little, Inc., 1978.

———. "Liberal Arts and Professional Ethics: Their Circuitous Connection." *Philosophical Reflections: Essays Presented to Dr. Norman E. Richardson.* Gettysburg, Pa.: Diablo Press, 1979.

Davis, John W., ed. *Contemporary Issues in Biomedical Ethics*. New Jersey: The Humana Press, Inc. 1978.

Dennis, K.J. and Hall, M.R.P. "The Teaching of Medical Ethics at Southhampton University Medical School," *Journal of Medical Ethics* 3 (December 1977): 183–85.

EVIST Resource Directory (Ethics and Values in Science and Technology), Washington, D.C.: Association for the Advancement of Science, 1978.

Gorovitz, Samuel. *Teaching Medical Ethics: A Report of One Approach*. Cleveland: Case Western Reserve University, 1973.

Human Values Teaching Programs for Health Professionals: Self-Descriptive Reports from Twenty-Nine Schools. 3rd Edition. Philadelphia: Society for Health and Human Values, 1976.

Jellinek, M. and Parmelee, D. "Is there a Role for Medical Ethics in Postgraduate Psychiatry Courses?" *American Journal of Psychiatry* 134 (December 1977): 1438–39.

Jones, J.S.P., and Metcalfe, D.H.H. "The Teaching of Medical Ethics in the Nottingham Medical School," *Journal of Medical Ethics* 2 (June 1976): 83–86.

Keller, Albert H., Jr. "Ethics/Human Values Education in The Family Practice Residency," *Journal of Medical Education* 52 (February 1977): 107–16.

Levine, Melvin D., et al. "Ethics Rounds in a Children's Medical Center: Evaluation of a Hospital-Based Program for Continuing Education in Medical Ethics," *Pediatrics* 60 (July 1977): 202–208.

Ministers in Medical Education: Seventy-Nine Self-descriptive Reports of the Work of Ministers in Health Education. Philadelphia: Society for Health and Human Values, 1979.

Pellegrino, Edmund. "Medical Ethics, Education, and The Physician's Image," *Journal of the American Medical Association* 235 (March 8, 1976): 1043–44.

———. *Humanism and the Physician*. Knoxville: University of Tennessee Press, 1979.

Purtilo, Ruth B. "Ethics Teaching in Allied Health Fields," *Hastings Center Report* 8 (April 1978).

Raths, L., Harmin, M., and Simon, S. *Values and Teaching: Working With Values in the Classroom*. Columbus, Ohio: Charles E. Merrill Publishing Co., 1966.

Rosen, Bernard. *Strategies of Ethics*. Boston: Houghton-Mifflin Co., 1978.

Sage, Smith, Fost, Boyd, and Kohlberg. *Teaching Biomedical and Health Care Ethics to Liberal Arts Undergraduates.* Chicago: Associated Colleges of the Midwest, 1977.

Self, Donnie J., ed. *The Role of the Humanities in Medical Education* Norfolk, Virginia: Teagle and Little, Inc., 1978.

Shetland, M.L. "The Responsibility of the Professional School for Preparing Nurses for Ethical, Moral, and Humanistic Practice," *Nursing Forum* 8 (1969): 17–28.

Siegler, Mark. "A Legacy of Osler: Teaching Clinical Ethics at the Bedside," *Journal of the American Medical Association* 239 (March 6, 1978): 951–56.

Steinfels, Margaret O'Brien. "Ethics, Education, and Nursing Practice," *Hastings Center Report* 7 (August 1977): 20–21.

Teaching of Bioethics: Report of the Commission on the Teaching of Bioethics. Hastings-on-Hudson, N.Y.: Institute of Society, Ethics and the Life Sciences, 1976.

"The Teaching of Ethics: A Preliminary Report," *Hastings Center Report* 7 (December 1977): A special supplement.

Veatch, Robert and Clouser, K. Danner. "New Mix in the Medical Curriculum," *Prism* 1 (November 1973): 62–66.

————, Gaylin, Willard. "Teaching Medical Ethics: An Experimental Program," *Journal of Medical Education* 47 (October 1972): 779–85.

————, Gaylin, W., and Morgan, C., eds. *The Teaching of Medical Ethics.* Hastings-on-Hudson, N.Y.: Institute of Society, Ethics and the Life Sciences, 1973.

Webb, Nancy, and Linn, Margaret. "Value Change During the First Year of Training: A Comparison of Medical, Nursing, and Social Work Students," *Journal of Medical Education* 51 (May 1976): 427–28.

2. Some Texts

The writings in the field of bioethics have become voluminous. What is suggested here are some means of entry into the field, not a library, just a vestibule. The list is primarily one of edited texts that deal with the central issues, using known articles, and giving further bibliography.

Another excellent route of entry is to become familiar with The

Hastings Center "Reading Series," which are packets of materials designed for student use. Their catalogue of packets is available from The Hastings Center, 360 Broadway, Hastings-on-Hudson, New York 10706.

Beauchamp, Tom, and Walters, LeRoy, eds. *Contemporary Issues in Bioethics.* Encino, Calif.: Dickenson Publishing Co., 1978.

Beauchamp, Tom, and Childress, James. *Principles of Biomedical Ethics.* New York: Oxford University Press, 1979.

"Bioethics and Social Responsibility," *The Monist* 60 (January 1977) entire issue.

Bliss, Brian P., and Johnson, Alan G. *Aims and Motives in Clinical Medicine: A Practical Approach to Medical Ethics.* London: Pitman Medical Publishing Co., Ltd., 1975 [Distributed by Beekman Publishers, 53 Park Place, New York, New York, 10007].

Brody, Howard. *Ethical Decisions in Medicine.* Boston: Little, Brown and Company, 1976.

Campbell, A.V. *Moral Dilemmas in Medicine.* Baltimore: The Williams Wilkins Company, 1972.

Clouser, K. Danner. "Bioethics," *Encyclopedia of Bioethics,* vol. 1, Warren T. Reich, ed. (New York: The Free Press), 1978.

———. "What Is Medical Ethics?" *Annals of Internal Medicine* 80 (May 1974): 657–60.

———. "Medical Ethics: Some Uses, Abuses, and Limitations," *New England Journal of Medicine* 293 (August 21, 1975): 384–87.

Davis, A., and Aroskar, M. *Ethical Dilemmas and Nursing Practice.* New York: Appleton-Century-Crofts, 1978.

Gorovitz, Samuel, et al., eds. *Moral Problems in Medicine.* Englewood Cliffs, N.J.: Prentice-Hall, 1976.

Humber, James M., and Almeder, Robert F., eds. *Biomedical Ethics and the Law.* New York: Plenum Press, 1976.

Hunt, Robert, and Arras, John, eds. *Ethical Issues in Modern Medicine.* Palo Alto, Calif.: Mayfield Publishing Company, 1977.

Jakobovits, Immanuel. *Jewish Medical Ethics.* New York: Bloch Publishing Company, 1959.

Munson, Ronald. *Intervention and Reflection: Basic Issues in Medical Ethics.* Belmont Calif.: Wadsworth, 1979.

Nelson, James B. *Human Medicine: Ethical Perspectives on New Medical Issues.* Minneapolis: Augsburg Publishing House, 1973.

Ramsey, Paul. *Ethics at The Edges of Life: Medical and Legal Intersections.* New Haven: Yale University Press, 1978.

————. *The Patient as Person.* New Haven: Yale University Press, 1970.

Reiser, S., Dyck, A., And Curran, W., eds. *Ethics in Medicine: Historical Perspectives and Contemporary Concerns.* Cambridge, Mass.: The M.I.T. Press, 1977.

Shannon, Thomas, ed. *Bioethics.* New York: Paulist Press, 1976.

Thomas, John, ed. *Matters of Life and Death.* Toronto: Samuel Stevens, 1978.

Vaux, Kenneth. *Biomedical Ethics: Morality for The New Medicine:* New York: Harper and Row, 1974.

Veatch, Robert M. *Case Studies in Medical Ethics.* Cambridge, Mass.: Harvard University Press, 1977.

Wertz, Richard W., ed. *Readings on Ethical and Social Issues in Biomedicine.* Englewood Cliffs, N.J.: Prentice-Hall, 1973.

Williams, Preston, ed. *Ethical Issues in Biology and Medicine.* Cambridge, Mass.: Schenkman Publishing Co., 1973.